IT HAPPENED TO ME

Series Editor: Arlene Hirschfelder

Books in the It Happened to Me series are designed for . . . itive teens digging for answers about certain illnesses, social issues, or lifestyle interests. Whether you are deep into your teen years or just entering them, these books are gold mines of up-to-date information, riveting teen views, and great visuals to help you figure out stuff. Besides special boxes highlighting singular facts, each book is enhanced with the latest reading list, websites, and an index. Perfect for browsing, there's loads of expert information by acclaimed writers to help parents, guardians, and librarians understand teen illness, tough situations, and lifestyle choices.

1. *Learning Disabilities: The Ultimate Teen Guide,* by Penny Hutchins Paquette and Cheryl Gerson Tuttle, 2003.
2. *Epilepsy: The Ultimate Teen Guide,* by Kathlyn Gay and Sean McGarrahan, 2002.
3. *Stress Relief: The Ultimate Teen Guide,* by Mark Powell, 2002.
4. *Making Sexual Decisions: The Ultimate Teen Guide,* by L. Kris Gowen, Ph.D., 2003.
5. *Asthma: The Ultimate Teen Guide,* by Penny Hutchins Paquette, 2003.
6. *Cultural Diversity: Conflicts and Challenges: The Ultimate Teen Guide,* by Kathlyn Gay, 2003.
7. *Diabetes: The Ultimate Teen Guide,* by Katherine J. Moran, 2004.
8. *When Will I Stop Hurting? Teens, Loss, and Grief: The Ultimate Teen Guide,* by Edward Myers, 2004.
9. *Volunteering: The Ultimate Teen Guide,* by Kathlyn Gay, 2004.
10. *How to Survive a Parent's Organ Transplant: The Ultimate Teen Guide,* by Tina P. Schwartz, 2004.

Volunteering

The Ultimate Teen Guide

KATHLYN GAY

It Happened to Me, No. 9

The Scarecrow Press, Inc.
Lanham, Maryland • Toronto • Oxford
2004

SCARECROW PRESS, INC.

Published in the United States of America
by Scarecrow Press, Inc.
A wholly owned subsidiary of
The Rowman & Littlefield Publishing Group, Inc.
4501 Forbes Boulevard, Suite 200, Lanham, Maryland 20706
www.scarecrowpress.com

PO Box 317
Oxford
OX2 9RU, UK

British Library Cataloguing in Publication Information Available

Library of Congress Cataloging-in-Publication Data

Gay, Kathlyn.
  Volunteering : the ultimate teen guide / Kathlyn Gay.
    p. cm. — (It happened to me ; no. 9)
  Includes bibliographical references and index.
  ISBN 978-0-8108-4922-8 (cloth : alk. paper); ISBN 978-0-8108-5833-6 (paper : alk. paper)
  1. Young volunteers. 2. Young volunteers in community development. 3.
Teenage volunteers in social service I. Title. II. Series.
HN49.V64G39 2004
361.3'7'0835—dc22
                                                        2004008174

⊗™ The paper used in this publication meets the minimum requirements of
American National Standard for Information Sciences—Permanence of
Paper for Printed Library Materials, ANSI/NISO Z39.48-1992.
Manufactured in the United States of America.

Contents

1 Being a Volunteer

In a Midwest city, teenagers with wheelbarrows moved hundreds of bricks from the remains of a run-down, two-story house in an eight-block area that had been cleared and landscaped for a public park. These volunteers from a high school building trades class laid the bricks by hand, row after row, to form a winding walkway through trees. More than a dozen years ago, they created a landmark that has been used ever since and will be there for years to come.

> Volunteering "helps people, and it shows that teens aren't always into violence."
> —member of a teen volunteer program in Clearwater, Florida[1]

Today, American young people who volunteer provide a great variety of services. For example:

◎ Teenagers help provide a humane sanctuary for abused and retired horses at Habitat for Horses in Galveston County, Texas. They not only care for horses but also help educate the public about animal abuse as well as horsemanship.

◎ During a recent summer, youth volunteers from all the high schools in Savannah, Georgia, worked eight hours a week for nine weeks in virtually every department at Memorial Health University Medical Center—from the children's hospital to the surgery center. The students worked one-on-one with doctors, nurses, and office staff, learning, as one volunteer noted "how to work in a hospital and . . . about the medical profession."[2]

◎ In numerous U.S. cities and towns teenage volunteers serve on a youth court, which hears misdemeanor offenses for juveniles aged 12 to 17 and provides a second chance for youth offenders without a criminal record. After pleading guilty, youth offenders are sentenced by a panel of their peers. The volunteer effort is demanding. Teens must spend a significant amount of time after school completing required training courses, and show up for court once a week.

◎ Teenage volunteers are indispensable in countless American communities where they help conduct fund-raisers for such organizations as the Juvenile Diabetes Association and the March of Dimes. They organize for cleanup projects in parks, vacant lots, and cemeteries; on beaches; and along rivers and streams. Teenagers volunteer to plant trees along parkways or at nature centers. They prepare meals for animals in zoos; they repair bicycles to distribute to kids who need them; they mentor young students who are struggling with reading or math; they help out with political campaigns (local, state, and national) and voter registration drives.

It's a Fact
The services teenagers provide each year as volunteers are worth more than $34 billion to the U.S. economy.

WHAT MAKES A SUCCESSFUL VOLUNTEER?

Leaders of volunteer programs often say that they look for certain qualities in individual youth who want to do some type of service work. These characteristics in random order include:

◎ Empathy and compassion
◎ Self-determination
◎ Commitment
◎ Reliability
◎ Willingness to collaborate with others
◎ Respect for confidentiality of beneficiaries
◎ Genuine desire to help others
◎ Enthusiasm and energy

A PERSONAL GLIMPSE

Although certainly not a requirement, in some instances a successful teenage volunteer has a background in service. Eighteen-year-old Christina Mahaus of Cincinnati, Ohio, is an example. She is a Leadership Development Counselor for the American Red Cross, but that is just one of her many efforts. As she explains: "I have been involved in some type of service work for as long as I can remember. . . . I became part of ACTS (Association of Christian Teenage Services), a service group for eighth-graders at my grade school and have been involved in many service clubs as well as doing service on my own ever since then."[3]

Besides teaching leadership skills in Red Cross classes, Mahaus has participated in a one-week service trip to South Texas called Project ARISE. "We held a summer camp for Mexican immigrant children," she says. In addition, she volunteers "one Thursday a month with my mom at Pregnancy Center West Distribution Center (a center that gives clothing and food to needy families while counseling and listening to the moms)." Her service also includes helping out at her church, volunteering at Mercy Franciscan Hospital, leading Girl Scout retreats, tutoring, and participating in fund-raisers.

Volunteer Christina Mahaus in Ohio packs supplies for a summer "Project ARISE" to help immigrant children in South Texas. Photo courtesy Christina Mahaus.

Christina has received numerous awards for her service, among them the Lighthouse Vision Award in 2003. But the recognition is not the main reward. She believes that volunteering has helped her find out what is "truly important in my life. . . . I always think I'm going to change someone's life, but normally my life is changed by those I am serving." As an example, she explains, "While in South Texas on the ARISE service trip we worked with people in severe poverty, but they came everyday with a smile on their faces, gave us a kiss on the cheek and were really happy to be there and be alive. They worked so hard to move up in the world, improve their homes and get an education. I really saw that I don't need to have a huge house or new clothes to be happy, all I really need is a great community, people that love me and a good disposition. I was reminded to look at the good and beautiful things in life."[4]

WHERE AND HOW YOUTH VOLUNTEER

While teenagers may be limited to certain types of tasks in some volunteer settings and are supervised by adults if they are minors, generally if you are aged 16 to 19 you can provide adult-type services through hundreds of regional or local branches of established organizations. These include such familiar names as the American Heart Association, American Red Cross, B'nai B'rith, Boy Scouts and Girl Scouts, Boys and Girls Club, 4-H, Humane Society, Youth Volunteer Corps, YM/YWCA, YM/YWHA, UNICEF, United Way, and many others. Local civic and religious groups also offer opportunities for volunteering.

If you want to volunteer you may also channel your volunteer efforts through "service learning" or "community service" courses offered at numerous elementary and secondary schools and colleges across the United States and Canada. In a trend that began several decades ago, students in community service courses learn by doing. That is, if you take such a course you can earn academic credits while applying what you learn in the classroom about real social, environmental, or economic problems in your community. In some cases, community service is a requirement for high school graduation, but surveys show that among young people a majority is opposed to this requirement.

EXPLORE SOME MORE

"Service-learning aims to build knowledge, character, and civic skills in young people by combining service to the community with academic learning," according to *Students in Service to America: A Guidebook for Engaging America's Students in a Lifelong Habit of Service*. Community service is integrated into a school's curriculum—"an after-school or community-based program can be linked to classroom academic instruction when teachers collaborate with the organizations sponsoring the program."

The guidebook points out that numerous organizations sponsor service programs, including the YMCA of the USA, Camp Fire USA, the United Cerebral Palsy Association, the National 4-H Council, the Points of Light Foundation and the Volunteer Center National Network, Youth Volunteer Corps of America, and America's Promise. "Service-learning programs can take many forms. They may take place during the school day, after school, on weekends, and/or during the summer. They may involve a single class or youth group, several classes, the whole school, or an entire school district."[5]

Nevertheless, community service provides needed work and at the same time allows teenagers to develop job skills and cultivate a sense of commitment—often a lifelong commitment—to making a positive impact in areas where they live.

Some youth take it upon themselves to set up their own service efforts. Consider 19-year-old Jessica Porter of Hudson, Florida, a small town north of Tampa. In May 2003, she and her longtime friend Ruthann Pleus began Operation Hometown Quilts, with the goal of stitching together quilts for all U.S. military families who have lost soldiers in the war on Iraq. That could mean hundreds of quilts.

Porter and Pleus had quilted together during their school years, until Pleus moved to Chicago. But the quilting project went on. Jessica's quilts with patriotic designs and colors are sent to families with a note: "With gratefulness for your sacrifice and devotion to freedom." A small, white patch on the back of the quilt reads: "Lovingly made by Jessica Porter."[7] Local quilters have also contributed to her project.

FROM THE BOOKSHELF

Catch the Spirit: Teen Volunteers Tell How They Made a Difference by social psychologist Susan K. Perry, Ph.D., includes "the personal stories of twenty otherwise perfectly typical teens who have given countless hours to start and run projects that help others," the author writes in her introduction. She points out: "Doing something because you want to, not because someone is grading you or paying you, is the best kind of motivation there is. It feels great!" Many of the teenagers, who have been honored with Prudential Spirit of Community Awards, use similar words to express their feelings about volunteering. The book also includes brief (one sentence) descriptions of projects by hundreds of other award winners.[6]

Porter's efforts were featured in a front-page story in the *New York Times* on September 3, 2003, and not long after the article was published Jessica and her mother Joanne, who helps with the quilting, began receiving quilt donations. For example, the Vienna Quilt Shop in Vienna, Virginia, sent six Amish quilts, which are valued for their hand stitching and colorful designs. No doubt the donations and the quilting operation in Florida will continue as long as the war in Iraq takes its toll in American lives.

WHO VOLUNTEERS?

Young people who volunteer come from diverse backgrounds and areas of the United States, and they provide a great variety of services. Teenager Clare Rosenfeld of Eugene, Oregon, for example, is a winner of one of the Prudential Spirit of Community Awards, a nationwide program honoring young people for outstanding acts of volunteerism. Clare received her award in 2003 for launching two organizations: one to raise public awareness of diabetes, and the other to educate, inspire, and support diabetic young people across the United States and worldwide. Another winner was 17-year-old Christopher Romero of Phoenix, Arizona, who survived a rough childhood and was inspired to develop a program that helps keep at-risk teens in his old school away from crime and drugs.[8]

Act Now
Start a school program to recognize students who have performed good deeds in the community or at their school.

Of course you don't have to be an award winner in order to provide valuable services. In fact, many youth give of their time and energy with no thought about "what's-in-it-for me," although they may reap intangible rewards such as greater self-esteem and self-confidence and pride in accomplishments.

Generally, young people volunteer at a rate higher than adults aged 26 and older. However, "efforts at measuring volunteering have produced widely different estimates, largely because of the methods employed to measure volunteering," reports the Center for Information & Research on Civic Learning & Engagement (CIRCLE). "For example, the Bureau of Labor Statistics' Current Population Survey estimated the national volunteer rate among adults age 16 and older at 27.6 percent in the year prior to September 2002. Alternatively, Independent Sector, a major source for information on volunteering and giving, reports a national volunteer rate of approximately 44 percent in 2000."[9] Overall, about 40 percent of youth report that they volunteered during 2002.

Student surveys conducted by Princeton, the University of Southern California, and other educational institutions show that teenagers are likely to volunteer if their parents are or have been volunteers and if they have done volunteer work when they were young children. These same students are more likely to become adult volunteers than those who did not volunteer at a younger age.

One survey for the University of Texas (UT) at Austin found that 74 percent of undergraduate students volunteered nearly three million hours in services during the academic year 2001–2002. Students reported volunteering because they wanted to help people in need or because volunteering gave them an opportunity to gain a new perspective on life. According to the survey findings, UT volunteerism "appears to be considerably higher than the nationwide percentage reflected by a December 2002 report by the U.S. Bureau of Labor Statistics. . . . It noted that 27.6 percent of the nation's civilian non-institutional population age 16 years and over volunteered through or for organizations at some point during the period from September 2001 to September 2002."[10]

> **Be Aware!**
> **Volunteering takes time, energy, and commitment and sometimes means giving up weekends or special events in order to provide services to others.**

Sly Majid is one UT volunteer who became involved with the University Volunteer Center, continuing the kind of volunteer work he had performed while in junior and senior high schools in his hometown of Allen, just north of Dallas. There he was active in United Way projects, worked in a community center, and mentored at elementary schools. His family values and Muslim faith have inspired him to seek volunteer opportunities. Volunteering is "something that has been a staple in my life and will be for many years to come," he says. "You should never wait for someone to do it for you. If you see a problem, go out there and try to fix it."[11]

Another UT volunteer, Ricardo Gutierrez of Hebbronville, Texas, says that for him volunteering is "not just something I can do, but something I should do." He, too, learned early in his life that it was important to help other people, a philosophy he carried with him when he entered the university.

FOLLOWING AN EXAMPLE

"Volunteerism was instilled in me at home, by my temple youth group in South Bend, Indiana, and B'nai B'rith Youth Organization (BBYO)," says Ellen Krulewitch of Elkhart, Indiana, as she recalls her years of service. Her parents first set the example. "They were such great volunteers when they lived in Chicago and then after they moved to Indiana; they especially helped to initiate the Sheltered Workshop for the disabled, later called the Association for the Disabled of Elkhart County(ADEC) Industries, and the association itself."

At the age of 15, Ellen volunteered at ADEC, helping a student who had severe developmental disabilities. "He was quite tall as I remember and often had seizures. We used to walk the outdoor grounds of the property with his hand on my shoulder so he knew I was there and wouldn't hurt him. Internally, I was worried he might hurt me, as he had been violent previously. But, he was quite kind, and although he didn't speak because he couldn't, we seemed to communicate."

Religious teachings also played a major part in inspiring Krulewitch's volunteerism. "Judaism teaches that we give of ourselves to help those less fortunate," she says. For example, she explained, "students at Temple Beth-El in South Bend who completed Confirmation in 10th grade generally become *madrichim*, or assistants to the teachers at religious school. They may do that for one or two years after completing religious school. Also, those who go through bar/bat mitzvah give a portion of their money gifts to a charity of some kind. It doesn't have to be a Jewish organization. It is a pledge that they realize the blessings bestowed upon them, and that it is good to give of themselves to an organization that will help others. It may be an animal rescue program, the Sierra Club, a homeless center, or one of hundreds of groups. It depends on the individual."

While in high school, Krulewitch took part in fund-raising activities and voter registration drives and in college volunteered for numerous campus volunteer efforts and at the Girls' Reform School outside of Indianapolis. "All of my volunteer experiences prompted me to eventually run for political office in Elkhart. Fortunately, I was elected three times as a city council person at-large, also the first Jewish person to serve the city as an at-large representative. I spent many hours working on city council issues and never thought my pay was one of the reasons to serve. It was an add-on to my commitment to community. As I was leaving the Elkhart City Council, I was bestowed with the highest honor for an Indiana citizen. I received the Sagamore of the Wabash designation with pin, plaque, and letter from [the late] Indiana Governor Frank O'Bannon. I was thrilled and appreciative of his generosity and kindness."[12]

NOTES

1. Theresa Blackwell, "Teen Volunteers Try to Make a Dent in Violence," *St. Petersburg Times*, July 18, 2001, electronic version, no page number.

2. Quoted in Philip Rucker, "Memorial Teen Volunteers Get Hands-On Training," *SAVVY*, August 2001, no page number, http://www.savannahnow.com/savvy/01features/0801volunteers.shtml (July 29, 2003).

3. Christina Mahaus, e-mail to the author, January 30, 2003.

4. Ibid.

5. "What Is Service Learning?" *Students in Service to America: A Guidebook for Engaging America's Students in a Lifelong Habit of Service* (Washington, D.C.: Corporation for National and Community Service, the U.S. Department of Education and the Points of Light Foundation and the Volunteer Center National Network with the USA Freedom Corps, 2002), 12.

6. Susan K. Perry, Ph.D., *Catch the Spirit: Teen Volunteers Tell How They Made a Difference* (New York: Julian Messner/Grolier, 2000).

7. Rebecca Catalanello, "Quilts a Patchwork of Emotion," *St. Petersburg Times*, September 8, 2003, Pasco Times section, 1. Also see Abby Goodnough, "Backing the Mission in Iraq, but Pondering Its Outcome," *New York Times,* September 3, 2003, 1.

8. Prudential Financial, "America's Top 10 Youth Volunteers Named in Eighth Annual Prudential Spirit of Community Awards," Press Release, May 5, 2003.

9. Mark Hugo Lopez, "Volunteering Among Young People," CIRCLE Fact Sheet, http://www.civicyouth.org/PopUps/frequency%20of%20volunteering.pdf (October 2, 2003).

10. University of Texas at Austin, "Volunteerism and Youth: Survey of Student Volunteerism at the University of Texas," April 2003.

11. Quoted in Office of Public Affairs, University of Texas at Austin, "Volunteering at the Heart of Student Experience," August 4, 2003, http://www.utexas.edu/features/archive/2003/volunteer2.html (August 5, 2003).

12. Ellen Krulewitch, e-mail to the author, August 3, 2003.

Building and Repairing

During their high school's mid-winter break in 2003, 80 teenagers from a church group in New Canaan, Connecticut, traveled to Dade City, Florida, to

> "Building a house sounds difficult, but it really is not that hard because you are not doing it all by yourself. You have help from other volunteers around your age. It [is] a joyful experience."—Jessica Velazquez, Habitat for Humanity volunteer

create a playground and soccer field for Farmworkers Self-Help, which provides services for some of the area's poorest families. Farmworkers had purchased the land for a park, and neighbors spent hours clearing away underbrush and garbage. But there was not enough money to build the park. So after learning about the problem, the Connecticut teenagers volunteered to do the work. They shared tasks with neighborhood young people, building a pavilion, creating a playground with a climbing wall and swings, and even painting a small house on the property. At the end of each day, they often shared meals with local families. One of the teenagers on the week-long project told a reporter that the experience was "great because you're seeing who you're doing this for."[1]

A year earlier, in 2002, another group of students made a trip during their spring break to Dade City to volunteer for Farmworkers Self-Help. They were participants in City Year, a national organization that brings together young people 17 to

24 years old to provide yearlong community services. The City Year volunteers came from De Anza College, San Jose City College, and San Jose State University in California, and were accompanied by six City Year employees. They spent 9- to 10-hour days working on a rundown duplex that Farmworkers had provided free to migrants working in the nearby farm fields. The building "looked like it had been abandoned for centuries. I didn't think any work could save the house," Scott Lillard, one of the volunteers, told a reporter. But after scrubbing and scraping paint, covering walls with new paint, putting up drywall, and performing other jobs, Lillard spoke for the group: "We were all amazed at the changes we made. . . . It had been transformed into a beautiful duplex."[2]

"IF I HAD A HAMMER"

Pete Seeger's well-known song "If I Had a Hammer" describes hammering all day long to show love and bring about justice. In many cases, you can do just that—if you pick up a hammer, saw, paint brush, or other tool to build or refurbish someone's home. In numerous American communities, teenagers may develop a park as the Connecticut students did, or create a play yard in a vacant lot with tire swings, sandboxes, and tree houses. More complex efforts involve renovating or building homes or other facilities from scratch. Usually professional construction workers (carpenters, brick layers, and the like) oversee major construction jobs, but a teen volunteer can participate within limits and under the direction of trades people.

There are also other volunteer opportunities for amateur builders. A youth group might seek the help of a building trades teacher, a volunteer bureau, or civic organization to establish a "handy helper" project in a low-income neighborhood or for the elderly. Jobs could include painting fences, repairing screens, building a wheelchair ramp or a yard platform to protect garbage cans from roaming dogs.

One youth group in the Midwest helped dismantle an entire house that was scheduled to be demolished so the land could be used for another purpose. The volunteer teens salvaged flooring, doors, windows, plumbing fixtures, hardware, and other materials for use in the restoration of another house in a different location.

In Oklahoma, shop students from Northwest Classen High School spent one day in April 2002 as part of a Handyman Program. They made repairs to an elderly widow's home in their neighborhood, completing an enclosed porch, installing a new front door, and adding some insulation.[3]

Act Now
Organize a group to publicize housing problems and pressure government officials to work for decent housing in all parts of your community.

A PERSONAL GLIMPSE

The project began with four teenage girls on the Crow Reservation in Montana. One of their teachers at Pretty Eagle Catholic School challenged them to work on a science project that would deal with a community problem. Knowing that many of their Crow tribe live in crowded mobile homes and flimsy government housing, the girls decided to tackle the problem of creating affordable, decent homes, using science to find a solution. Their teacher encouraged them to visit a nearby straw-bale home in Crow country built by a nonprofit volunteer group called the Red Feather Development Group headquartered in Seattle, Washington.

Bales of straw to construct a home? It seemed unbelievable. An old fable, after all, tells of the big bad wolf blowing down a house of straw. But straw-bale construction is durable and dates back thousands of years. After the girls from Pretty Eagle saw first hand the structure of the straw-bale home in Crow country, they designed a science project to demonstrate that straw bales covered with stucco are not only waterproof, but also fire resistant. Then they entered their experiment in a national competition that brought them a grand prize of $25,000 plus a similar grant from TV star and talk show hostess Oprah Winfrey.

The girls donated the money to build a community study hall, which has multiple purposes, from computer classes to senior gatherings. The Red Feather group designed the building and about three dozen volunteers—including the girls who were on the site almost daily—built the structure in about 18 days. Since then, the teenagers have planned other projects to benefit their community.[4]

EXPLORE SOME MORE

In the late 1800s, it was common to build homes using bales of straw in timber-poor Nebraska, but as wood and other supplies became more readily available through improved transportation, straw-bale construction was no longer popular. Straw-bale building was revived in North America in the 1980s, and today such buildings can be found in various parts of the Southwest (as well as in other countries). See http://www.ems.org/straw_bale/intro.html, http://www.epsea.org/straw.html, and http://www.greenbuilder.com/sourcebook/strawbale.html

HABITAT BUILDING PROGRAMS

One of the most widely known volunteer building programs that constructs homes from the ground up is Habitat for Humanity International (HHI), which calls itself "an ecumenical Christian ministry dedicated to eliminating poverty housing." The group includes people of many faiths. In Glencoe, Illinois, for example, Glencoe Interfaith Builders (GIB) is working with Habitat. Representatives of eight congregations are committed to help build a Habitat House: Am Shalom, Congregation Hakafa, Glencoe Union Church, North Shore Congregation Israel, North Shore United Methodist Church, Sacred Heart Catholic Church, Saint Elisabeth Episcopal Church, and Saint Paul African Methodist Episcopal Church. But a volunteer does not have to belong to one of the congregations in order to participate, and minors age 16 to 18 who sign liability waivers are welcome, the group says. In collaboration with Habitat, they plan to build duplexes (about 25 homes) in the Carter Woods subdivision of Waukegan, Illinois.

Wherever Habitat homes are built, prospective owners are required to provide some labor—"sweat equity" as it's called—along with the volunteers. Teenagers who volunteer have to be 18 years of age or older to work on actual construction, but 16- and 17-year-olds are allowed with parental/guardian permission to be on a building site to perform various jobs under supervision—perhaps carrying bricks or concrete blocks or pushing a wheelbarrow full of concrete.

During the summer of 2003, for example, about three dozen young people aged 16 to 18 from 27 states were part of a "summer youth blitz" to build a house at each of two sites:

Be Aware!
Construction jobs can be physically tiring, dirty, and sweaty work, so if that's not appealing try another type of volunteering.

Cookeville, Tennessee, and Belen, New Mexico. Jessica Velazquez of Brooklyn, New York, was one of the volunteers who flew to New Mexico to work on a Habitat project for a two-week period during the summer of 2003. She says she learned about the program from a Habitat newsletter that her mother receives. She reports, "I already had some building experience" but had never participated in a volunteer program like Habitat. "I could not even begin to imagine what I would experience during the two weeks." Although a bit apprehensive at first, she was excited about the opportunity to volunteer. It became a learning period. As Jessica explains:

> I learned how to be patient and how to work hard with a team of people to fulfill a common goal. . . . I also learned some

Jessica Velazquez, a Habitat for Humanity volunteer, poses atop a house under construction in New Mexico. Photo courtesy Jessica Velazquez.

construction skills that I knew would come in handy. I became great friends with people at the site. I have learned so much from the experience that it will be with me forever. I feel like I've grown so much and appreciate life more. I would definitely recommend this type of volunteerism to other teens. Habitat for Humanity is a great organization and the people that you meet are wonderful—especially the leaders! They were not only leaders but friends. They made sure we had activities to do in the afternoon after work. We went to the pool to relax. . . . At night before quiet hour we had discussions about how everyone's day was. . . . The leaders always made sure that any conflicts were resolved and they made sure that we had everything that we needed and that we were able to talk to our family throughout the two weeks that we were in New Mexico. . . . I would participate [again] in Habitat for Humanity in a heartbeat.[5]

Students from the University of California Santa Barbara (UCSB) also have taken part in Habitat for Humanity projects. During their spring break in 2003, they traveled north to Portland, Oregon, to build a house for a low-income family. "We wanted to do something meaningful with our break," noted Sarah Crowley, president of the UCSB chapter of Habitat. "It felt good to spend our time in a positive way."[6] Prior to their Portland project, the UCSB students worked on home building in Texas and New Mexico. In addition, the students also work two weekends each month with Habitat on buildings in nearby communities.

Examples of where and how Habitat volunteers work are readily available on the Internet. Just the search term "Habitat for Humanity" will provide access to hundreds of sites describing projects and locations.

REPAIRING AND REHABILITATING

Instead of building new homes, numerous volunteer groups in nearly all regions of the United States apply their efforts to rehabilitate existing structures. One example is the Southern Missouri Project (SOMOPRO) in New Madrid, Missouri. Sister Marie Orf of St. Vincent's Parish in Chicago is the main organizer of this volunteer project, which is sponsored by the

IT'S A FACT

A famous Habitat for Humanity volunteer is former U.S. President Jimmy Carter. Because he has led many work projects for Habitat, Carter is sometimes mistakenly called the founder of the organization. However, the group was initiated in 1976 by millionaire businessman Millard Fuller and his wife Linda. Fuller gave away much of his fortune to people in need and set up a Christian housing ministry, although people of all faiths participate. In 2003, the *NonProfit Times* named Fuller "Executive of the Year." Habitat now has affiliates in more than 3,000 communities in 89 nations.

Roman Catholic Vincentian Community, Sisters of the Most Precious Blood, and other benefactors.

SOMOPRO brings together volunteers—usually Catholic— from the Midwest and other parts of the nation to refurbish homes of low-income residents in the "boot heel" of Missouri. About three dozen volunteers participate during a six-day work week in the summer. Most of the volunteers are high school students or young people in their twenties. They pay a $25.00 registration fee to help cover the costs of travel and food, and stay in a parish school in Madrid, Missouri.

During their 2003 effort, the SOMOPRO volunteers put new roofs on four homes and painted five others. Sister Marie reported that while they were painting one of the houses, "an elderly lady . . . came to us in the afternoon with this question: 'How poor do you have to be to get your house painted?' Her question surely touched our hearts."[7] The woman's house was scheduled for the next painting project.

World Changers (WC) is a faith-based organization that encourages teenagers to participate in volunteer construction projects. Initiated by Southern Baptists in 1990, WC focuses on refurbishing homes in central city neighborhoods. During the summer of 2002, for instance, the Southwest Baptist Theological Seminary in Fort Worth, Texas, invited WC volunteers—many of them high school and college students—to rehabilitate 26 homes in the city. A city housing director identified homes needing repairs and provided some construction materials.

A religious organization called Group Workcamps with headquarters in Loveland, Colorado, sends teenaged volunteers out to provide free home repairs for the elderly, handicapped, and low-income residents across the United States during June, July, and August. In 2002, more than 20,000 teenagers participated in 26 communities through this interdenominational Christian group. "Teenagers say the work can be a life-changing experience. Through teamwork, determination, [and] small acts of kindness," volunteering prompts young people "to continue similar efforts elsewhere in [their] life," says Joe Curry, Workcamp volunteer.[8]

A national nonsectarian, nonprofit group which began as "Christmas in April" and is now known as Rebuilding Together has been operating since 1988, organizing volunteers willing to help their low-income neighbors maintain their homes. With headquarters in Washington, D.C., and more than 250 affiliates, Rebuilding Together volunteers, many of them teenagers, serve in hundreds of communities across the United States. Homeowners receive services and supplies free of charge. According to the organization, the homes selected for repairs are owned by low-income residents who are elderly, disabled, or families with children, and are unable to do the work themselves. "The site selection process takes place locally, within broad national guidelines. Criteria differ slightly from affiliate to affiliate. Individual families are referred through neighborhood associations, churches, synagogues, community organizations, and service groups, or by self-referral."[9]

It's a Fact

The number of low-income homeowners in the United States increases each year, from approximately 22 million low-income homeowner families in 2003 to an estimated "28.5 million by the year 2010. This growth means that more and more families are placed in the position of choosing between vital necessities, such as food or medicine, or a roof that does not leak."
—About Rebuilding Together

A PERSONAL GLIMPSE

Tens of thousands of Rebuilding volunteers provide millions of hours of work each year to rehabilitate homes. One of those rebuilders is Megan Sherman of Seattle, Washington, who has been involved as a volunteer since her freshman year in high school. She joined the youth program, a pioneering effort of the organization. "That particular year, we had several youth sites (ones designated to be repaired mostly by high school students)," she says. "It was a youth home and many of the volunteers worked side by side with the residents. It was a very fun experience, and I gained so much knowledge in a single day, learning from other volunteers as well as the adult house captains. By the end of the day I felt like a handy woman extraordinaire! I was gardening, painting, removing tree stumps and attaching door handles."[10]

By the end of her sophomore year Megan was looking for other ways to become involved in Rebuilding Together. She began serving on the Youth Advisory Board, and when two of her friends on the board left for college, she worried a bit about organizing a Rebuilding Day for 2003. But, she says, after sites were selected for youth volunteers, "we began recruiting at our schools, rounding up as many volunteers as we could. As always, Rebuilding Day is a blast! Its so much fun to really get in there and get dirty, scraping paint, tearing down overgrown bushes, it's a kind of satisfaction that is heightened by the fact that it is all for someone who was unable to do it themselves. Each year it is so rewarding to see the look of appreciation from the homeowner. That must be one of my favorite parts of the whole operation. Now, as I leave for college I am looking for a way to become involved in Spokane, Washington, while I attend Gonzaga University."[11]

NOTES

1. Quoted in Bridget Hall Grumet, "On a Seedy Lot, 80 Teens Work a Miracle for Nonprofit Group," *St. Petersburg Times,* February 20, 2003, Pasco Times Section, 1.

2. Quoted in Jennifer Zhang, "Students Spend Spring Break Building Hope," *The Cupertino Courier,* May 1, 2002, http://www.svcn.com/archives/cupertinocourier/05.01.02/city-year-0218.html (August 8, 2003).

3. "Handyman Program Rebuilds Neighborhoods," *The Daily Oklahoman,* April 11, 2002, http://www.rebuildingtogether.org/news _information/Publications/oklahoman.htm (August 6, 2003).

4. Michelle Nijhuis, "Crow Girls' Winning Science Project is Not the Last Straw," *The Christian Science Monitor,* August 20, 2002, http://www.csmonitor.com/2002/0820/p16s01-lecs.html (August 9, 2003).

5. Jessica Velazquez, e-mail to the author, August 23, 2003.

6. Quoted in Drew Atkins, "Students Head North to Build Homes for Poor," *Daily Nexus Online,* April 10, 2003, http://www.dailynexus.com/news/2003/4886.html (August 9, 2003).

7. Sister Marie, St. Vincent DePaul Parish, "Summer Volunteer Work—For Those Who Love to Work!" no date, http://www.stvdep .org/somopro/index.asp (August 15, 2003).

8. Religion News Service, "20,000 Teenagers Descend Upon 62 Communities This Summer to Help Rebuild America," press release, Summer 2002, http://www.religionnews.com/press02/PR061302B .html (August 21, 2003).

9. "About Rebuilding Together" no date, http://www .rebuildingtogether.org/about_rebuilding_together/index .shtml (August 15, 2003).

10. Megan Sherman, e-mail to the author, August 11, 2003.

11. Ibid.

Closing the Generation Gap

Helping elderly citizens with building or repair projects is only one of many volunteer activities that young people provide for seniors. However,

> "I help . . . with activities for the residents [of a nursing home]. We have card clubs, cooking classes, and even hold basketball tournaments. I used to think something like this would be boring and uncomfortable but I enjoy volunteering. They are all really nice people, and I have gotten close to some of them."—Sarah H. of Auburn, New York[1]

working and sharing with senior citizens is actually a two-way street, a give-and-take process, which helps close the gap between young and old. That gap has widened considerably over the last few decades.

In the past, it was common for several generations to participate together in many activities, and in some cultures that is still true. But today extended American families are often separated by distance and differences in life styles. Young and old are also segregated by age. Generations United, an organization that promotes programs and policies to close the generation gap, explains: "Children attend age-segregated schools; adults work in environments almost exclusive of children under 16 and adults over 65; older adults often live in senior only housing; and both children and older persons are cared for in single age-use facilities (day or long-term care). Furthermore, too few American institutions bring together people of different ages, backgrounds, abilities, races, and ethnicities in a common cause. Both young people and older adults suffer from a sense of isolation."[2]

If you are willing to help older people you will be in great demand, primarily because the number of American elderly is constantly increasing. With a longer life span, people may have health problems, or experience difficulty finding transportation, maintaining homes, or just communicating with others. Sometimes older people are able to maintain their independence if they get help with a few simple tasks.

WHAT YOUTH VOLUNTEERS CAN DO

Volunteer programs providing services for seniors are known by a variety of names, from "Adopt a Grandparent" (volunteering to be with and treat an elderly person just like a grandparent) to "Youth–Elderly Pen Pals" (corresponding with an older person by postal or e-mail). These activities may take place in nursing homes; senior citizen and retirement communities; places of worship; community, park, and recreation centers; libraries; and individual homes.

The activities and projects listed below have been compiled from the successful experiences of various youth groups, and can easily be adapted by an individual, small group, or volunteer organization:

- *Make Telephone Calls.* **Sometimes calling senior citizens who live alone and have few if any visitors can brighten a day. A little small talk every now and then also helps young people communicate their concern.**
- *Provide Light Housekeeping.* **For senior citizens who have difficulty getting around, volunteers can make up beds, carry out trash, wash dishes, sweep or vacuum, or do other jobs that require mobility.**
- *Post-a-Note.* **Ask senior citizens living in high-rise buildings or nursing homes to tack up "help wanted" notices on a central bulletin board. Volunteers can respond with appropriate services.**
- *Form a "Signal Corps."* **Help seniors create posters, flags, or other signs that older folks can put in windows or on doors of their homes to signal that they need assistance from one of a**

corps of young volunteers who patrol an area where elderly people live.

◎ *Compile a Date Book.* List birthdays and special occasions for senior citizens and remember them with cards or small gifts.

◎ *Establish a Messenger Service.* Mail letters, pay bills, or pick up groceries, library books, prescriptions, and so forth, for seniors.

◎ *Create a Senior Living Guide.* Research and compile a list of the social services (agencies and programs) that assist senior citizens in the local area. Describe what services are available—who to contact, how to apply for aid—or provide whatever practical information is needed.

◎ *Organize a Cooking Club.* Set up regular cooking demonstrations so seniors can share recipes, skills, and helpful kitchen hints with young volunteers. Compile a cookbook of favorite, "old-time"(hand-me-down) recipes.

◎ *Have an Arts and Crafts Fair.* Display and sell the work of elderly citizens. Older folks might teach young people how to quilt, do wood carving, or garden.

◎ *Promote a Living History Day/Week.* Help seniors write up memorable events in their lives that could be put together in booklet form. Display antique furniture, old trinkets, books, dishes, and other items from the past in a community center, library, or other public place. Plan publicity or special events to call attention to those in the community who can describe "the way it was."

◎ *Provide Transportation or Escort Services.* Take older folks to religious services, shopping centers, libraries, meetings, service centers, agencies, doctor's offices, or on other errands. Providing transportation for seniors who want to visit friends or family is a great help too.

◎ *Read Aloud.* Visit elderly people who may have poor eyesight or simply don't have much reading material, and read books or articles aloud. This activity is often enjoyable for both the recipient and the reader.

◎ *Make Greeting Cards.* Involvement can be on a one-time, occasional, or ongoing basis. Cards can be made by individuals at home or with a group, then mailed to elderly shut-ins.

By volunteering to help seniors, young people say they learn that there is an entirely different way of looking at the

Act Now
Raise awareness of senior citizen needs through news releases, newsletters, letters to or discussions with local politicians.

world. At age 70 or 80, one does not have the same views as someone 17 or 18. "Working with the elderly proved to be a very sobering experience," as one volunteer put it. Teens also express excitement and pleasure when they discover the heritage of their community through their elders.

WHAT ARE INTERGENERATIONAL PROGRAMS?

Simply put, they are an effort—usually volunteer projects —that bring young and old together to provide benefits for the community and at the same time share with and support one another. Organizers of intergenerational programs usually advise youth volunteers to do things *with* the elderly, rather than just *for* them. That also is a basic recommendation for seniors. In other words, participants are trained to be sensitive to one another and part of that sensitivity training could be a discussion about stereotypes that each age group has about the other and ways to overcome those stereotypes.

IT'S A FACT

Many older adults believe that teenagers are lazy, selfish hooligans, and that young people are primarily interested in "hanging out," watching TV, and playing video games. That myth is discredited by statistics showing that in recent years the number of teenagers who volunteer to help others has increased dramatically.

Just as older people may stereotype teenagers, younger people may also stereotype the elderly, labeling them as needy, feeble, dependent, frightened, lonely, and poor—or affluent, self-centered, grumpy, and intolerant. Intergenerational programs frequently debunk such negative images.

To assure that intergenerational programs will be successful, students and seniors need plenty of opportunities to get to know each other, share feelings, and develop trust, advisors say. A most important factor is making an activity enjoyable.

In some cases, training sessions are held for students

EXPLORE SOME MORE

Intergenerational programs include such benefits as

- Encouraging the older generation to pass on traditions and values to younger people.
- Fostering relationships between young and old.
- Reducing alienation between generations.
- Helping dispel inaccurate stereotypes.
- Strengthening communities by helping people connect with one another.
- Improving communication skills of young and old alike.

More about intergenerational programs can be found on the Generations United website (www.gu.org).

and seniors in volunteer programs. The emphasis is on respect for one another as *individuals* and being genuinely interested in each other's views, needs, and feelings.

Intergenerational programs are often part of 4-H Club and Future Homemakers of America activities. Volunteers are trained to provide a variety of assisted-living services and those who receive services reciprocate by sharing their time and talents with the volunteers; in this way youth learn about the aging process and both generations learn to communicate with one another.

The Retired Senior Volunteer Program (RSVP) also fosters intergenerational programs. RSVP and teen volunteers may be members of a team working in elementary schools. They may

Be Aware!
Some elderly people are extremely lonely and like to talk and talk when volunteers visit; good listening and patience are a must for this type of volunteer service.

A PERSONAL GLIMPSE

In Manatee County, Florida, the ManaTEEN Club, the largest, locally based teen volunteer program in the United States with more than 10,000 members, began a short-term project in 1999 to help senior citizens prepare for the hurricane season. The ManaTEENS surveyed their own neighborhoods throughout Manatee and Sarasota counties where many senior citizens live and found that more than 7,000 elderly were living alone, sometimes in poorly maintained homes, with no family members nearby. As a result the teenagers organized a project to deliver emergency meals and flashlight kits to the seniors.

Since 1999, the program has expanded and now addresses broader safety concerns that older citizens may face. Called Home Safety for Seniors, the program is sponsored by Lowe's, the home improvement company, and its Home Safety Council. ManaTEEN volunteers visit homes to learn about safety needs in senior homes, marking items on an inventory list. Lowe's provides the supplies to benefit a needy senior, then with adult supervision volunteers deliver and/or install items such as smoke alarms, bathtub safety rails, anti-slip floor mats, window and door locks, and peep-holes.

Lowe's personnel train ManaTEENS on how to correctly install safety items. In addition the volunteers receive sensitivity training. During the course, they wear special glasses to simulate eye diseases such as cataracts, which blur vision. They also use special gloves to learn what it is like to try to do tasks when arthritis makes fingers stiff. The training helps students better understand the needs of people they visit. Because of the success of the ManaTEENS efforts, the Senior Safety program is now under way in other parts of the United States in cities like Los Angeles and Las Vegas.

conduct after-school programs, teaching such topics as health and safety awareness skills to kindergarten and early elementary students. Through such efforts RSVP volunteers become valued and trusted mentors to the young people who serve with them.

Other intergenerational programs may provide such services as respite to families caring for frail elders, delivering Meals-on-Wheels, working with older adults in museum or arts programs, participating in environmental preservation projects, or being part of an intergenerational orchestra.

BONDING WITH VETERANS

One special way that teen volunteers close the gap between themselves and the older generation is by taking part in programs for America's veterans. According to the Veterans Administration (VA), "Nationally, the number of VA student volunteers has increased dramatically, from under 10,000 in 1995 to approximately 24,000 in 2001. . . . Student volunteers bring energy and enthusiasm into the medical center that crosses generations and touches the hearts of hospitalized veterans."[3]

Some of those volunteers are in Houston, Texas. In 2002, for example, 20 Medical Science Academy students from Hightower High School volunteered at the VA Medical Center. During the school year, they served three days a week, every other week.

In Florida, a volunteer program for veterans began with Philip Nodhturft and his recruits from the Jesuit High School in Tampa. Nodhturft initiated a chess and checkers club at the VA Nursing Home. Why did he want to work with veterans? "All my grandfathers, all the way back to the Civil War, were full-time military officers," he explained. "I have a special spot in my heart for veterans who have diligently served our country. They are our true heroes. For those reasons, I chose the Tampa VA nursing home to do my volunteer work."[4]

The club that Nodhturft started meets once each week and has been highly successful with the veterans. It has grown from 10 student volunteers to more than 40, and has helped students and elderly veterans cultivate positive relationships as they talk and share experiences between moves on the game board. VA volunteer program directors say that young people "bring a special new air of freshness that brightens the nursing home. . . . Often they enhance the morale of older veterans, especially those who have no visitors."[5]

As for Nodhturft's assessment: "Both generations bonded with each other. The veterans felt linked with the outside community as they connected with us, and we looked forward to serving because it was fun and we enjoyed listening to the veterans interesting and funny stories. A special relationship developed that's hard to describe. It was the mutual respect we had for each other that made it special. I realize now that I can really make a difference in the lives of others just by taking a few hours a week out of my schedule. . . . I have come to view my community service as [a] responsibility and not something I do when and if I have time. I make time."[6]

NOTES

1. Sarah H., "Volunteers Have That Magic Touch," *Teen Ink*, October 1999, http://teenink.com/Past/9900/October/Community/ Volunteers.html (October 2, 2003).

2. Generations United, "Statement Submitted to the United States Environmental Protection Agency May 7, 2003 Listening Session," http://www.epa.gov/aging/listening/2003/balt_dbutts.pdf (August 19, 2003).

3. Veterans Administration, "Houston VA Medical Center Volunteers Exemplify True American Spirit," press release, April 17, 2002, http://www.houston.med.va.gov/pressreleases/news_ 20020417b.html (August 17, 2003).

4. Quoted in "Building Better Lives for America's Disabled Veterans," *Disabled American Veterans (DAV) Magazine*, March–April 2000, 73, http://www.dav.org/magazine/magazine_ archives/2000-2/Youth_Volunteers1417_print.html (August 16, 2003).

5. Ibid.

6. Ibid.

4 Helping with Health Care

Like the teen volunteers who work in VA medical centers, those who help out in other community health-care facilities not only are caring individuals but also seem to have special qualities such as

> "In addition to talking with patients about their childhoods, how they have been feeling, and their own families, I attempt to interact with them through activities they seem to enjoy."—Emily Tibbets[1]

patience and often a desire to someday become a professional in a medical field. If that's your bent, where would you volunteer? Some of the possibilities include general hospitals, chronic disease facilities, nursing homes, psychiatric treatment centers, physical rehabilitation centers, and hospice programs. The services health-care volunteers provide are always determined by specific needs, but here are a few categories and descriptions of jobs filled by teen volunteers:

1. **Nursing Services**
   - ◎ **make beds**
   - ◎ **feed patients**
   - ◎ **fill water pitchers**
2. **Personal Services**
   - ◎ **give manicures**
   - ◎ **read to patients**

- write letters
- interpret for non-English-speaking patients
- be a friendly visitor

3. Therapy (occupational and physical) Services
   - teach exercises
   - push wheelchairs
   - make slings, contour pillows, and other aids for physically handicapped
   - assist with arts and crafts projects
   - maintain various types of equipment, organize supplies, materials
   - help with games and play music

4. Dietary Services
   - make up trays
   - carry meals
   - help seat disabled at tables

5. Recreational Services
   - plan, organize games or parties
   - direct sports
   - sponsor dance, theater groups, other programs
   - teach music, plan concerts or singing groups

6. Escort, Messenger, Delivery Services
   - escort patients on shopping tours or to special events from health-care facilities
   - deliver mail and flowers to patients and inter-office memos
   - operate library and/or gift carts
   - take patients to and from rooms
   - act as tour guide
   - carry supplies

7. Clerical
   - work in various departments such as pharmacy, x-ray, dietary
   - catalog, sort, and review books in library

Act Now
Serve as a volunteer HIV/AIDS outreach worker for a community center or other institution, helping to raise awareness of HIV testing at street fairs, college fairs, and other community-based events.

A PERSONAL GLIMPSE

"Heavenly Hats" is the name teenager Anthony Leanna of Suamico, Wisconsin, created for his volunteer program, which he initiated in 2001 to help cancer patients. What do hats have to do with cancer? They are attractive head coverings for people who have lost their hair due to chemotherapy treatments. (He accepts only new hats because of the patients' weakened immune systems.) Inspiring stories about Anthony's program have appeared in publications across the United States, especially after he won an award in 2002 from the Points of Light Foundation, a nonprofit organization promoting volunteerism that the elder President Bush established. But Anthony's own words best explain his efforts:

I started . . . "Heavenly Hats" after my grandma had breast cancer and I saw a lot of people in the hospitals without hair because of their cancer treatments and just wanted them to feel better about themselves. I was about 9 years old at the time. I wasn't sure how I was going to help, but I thought about it for several months when the idea of giving the patients new hats to wear when they are in the hospital came to me. It was over Easter Break from school and I didn't want to spend my whole break sitting around watching TV, I wanted to do something to help these people.

I sat down at my computer and made up signs and taped them to boxes. My signs were asking for new hat donations for cancer patients. My mom drove me to different businesses in my hometown where I talked to store managers and asked them if I could put my boxes in their stores. Most of them were more than willing to help, and I would go back there once a week to collect the hats that were donated. I was able to start providing a few hats to local hospitals in my hometown.

Soon the media [began publicizing] my idea and donations really started to come in. Then I had the idea to e-mail hat companies and bandanna companies around the world and ask for donations and many companies started sending me their extras or flawed hats. I then was able to start contacting hospitals in other states and mailing out hats to them. To date I have shipped more than 14,000 new hats to over 70 different hospitals and clinics.

(continued)

31

A PERSONAL GLIMPSE (Continued)

I have received hats from as far away as Australia. I bag each hat individually and box them according to the type of hospital that I am shipping to. If I am sending to a children's hospital I try and send only kids and teen type hats. When I started this program I thought I was only going to be able to help a few local cancer patients and now my program has grown and I am able to help thousands.

It makes me feel so good inside when I receive a thank you note or phone call from some of the patients who said that the hat meant so much to them. Many of them say the hat is a symbol of hope because they know that there is someone out there that they have never met who actually cares about them. I have received many awards for my program, but the biggest award is being able to put a smile on the faces of people who are going through a really hard time in their lives. My grandma, grandpa and dad have cancer and it is a very hard thing to go through, so anything that people can do to help really makes a difference during these hard times.

I thought being a kid that I would never be able to make such a difference, but with a little imagination and effort I was able to. I think many people especially kids think that their efforts won't really help so they don't do anything at all. I have found that even a little thing such as a hat can make a big difference in the lives of thousands.[2]

More information about "Heavenly Hats" is provided on Anthony's website (http://www.heavenlyhats.com) or by contacting him at HEAVENLY HATS, 1813 Coach Lane, Suamico, WI 54173.

PLACING STUDENT VOLUNTEERS

If you want to volunteer in health care you can go directly to a facility, but more likely you would work through a school service-learning program, an organization like the American Red Cross or Epilepsy Foundation of America. You could also contact a city or county health department, where, for example, volunteers may help with a lead testing clinic by teaching primary students about lead poisoning and publicizing free lead tests with posters, newspaper articles, and flyers. During the testing day, volunteers may escort children from their classrooms, help mothers entertain preschoolers who are waiting for tests, and fill out laboratory forms.

Community service programs required for high school graduation help place numerous students in volunteer health-care facilities. A high school sophomore, Sarah Homerding, is one of 25 such volunteers at Silver Cross Hospital in Joliet, Illinois, where teenagers are escorts guiding patients around the

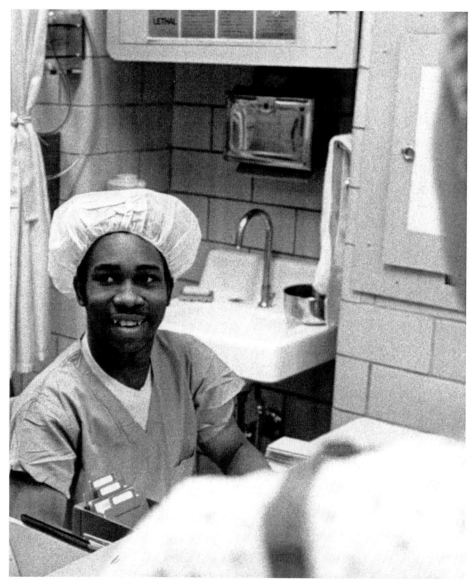

A teen volunteer helps out with clerical work in a Chicago hospital. Photo courtesy
Mt. Sinai Hospital.

hospital, assistants on the pediatric floor, clerks in a variety of
departments, and receptionists. In Homerding's view, "Silver
Cross is flexible, so I can find time for volunteering on
weekends" when she works from 8:00 A.M. to 12:30 P.M. on
Saturdays in the Diagnostic Department Reception Room. She
signs in patients and talks to them, "and you listen," she says.
"I feel like I've really done something to help people."[3]

The American Red Cross is well known for placing volunteer teens in health care and training them in health and safety skills such as first aid, swimming and water safety, lifeguarding, and CPR. Teenagers also learn how to prepare for disasters and assist in disaster shelters. In addition, they take part in blood donation drives. A local chapter no doubt has a variety of volunteer jobs for youth.

Marilyn is a composite of numerous Red Cross volunteers, who start out in middle school learning about first aid and water safety. Then in about ninth grade Marilyn got into a Red Cross program for the elderly and went to a nursing home where she wrote letters for people. Some of the residents thought of her as their grand-daughter and she got to know their families through the mail. She also helped with game activities. The following year she became a hospital volunteer, working in the lab and in surgery areas as a courier and carrying messages back and forth. Marilyn eventually went to college, where she studied for a nursing career.

Red Cross youth leaders say they work especially hard to see that health care facilities have specific volunteer job descriptions for teens. Leaders do not want to send teenagers to a hospital telling them they'll have "a really neat learning experience" and then those teenagers find themselves in a basement folding sheets. In short, the Red Cross says it wants to place teens in jobs that are significant to them and provide real services for an agency or institution.

EXPLORE SOME MORE

A cross is often used as a religious symbol, but that is not the case with the American Red Cross. Nevertheless, some people view it that way. So in most Islamic countries, a red crescent is used instead of the red cross and in Israel, the Magen David Adom, or Red Shield of David, is the symbol used.[4]

Be Aware!
Sometimes volunteer work in health-care facilities may require jobs considered unpleasant—emptying bed pans, for example, or helping to feed or bathe patients.

TRAINING

In most health-care facilities, teen volunteers are usually not assigned until they receive some type of training. Training beforehand is extremely important when volunteers serve at psychiatric treatment centers. In some training sessions, students learn expressive techniques that help in self-understanding and patient activities. Perhaps they make self-image collages, paint to music, and go through many nonverbal exercises to express themselves without sound or words. Volunteers may work with psychiatric patients in activities such as group paint-ins—an entire group painting on a huge sheet of paper spread on the floor. This can help patients express fears and relieve anxieties or even vent anger. Patients learn to express positive emotions like joy this way too.

In some cases, it can be frightening to be with patients who shout and swear or express anger in other ways. Volunteers can easily assume that such a patient might attack them. But they learn not to take things personally. Frequently patients are simply trying to find out what is happening to them and need help working things out because they can't cope.

When teenage volunteers participate in programs for physically or mentally challenged children, a psychologist and therapist provide training for the volunteers, explaining about physical therapy, proper handling of retarded youngsters, and various teaching methods. Volunteers in such program are regularly supervised and often work in teams, reporting to a hospital or facility one day every week or two. Some of their tasks include setting up tape players for children involved in a sound stimulation program, assisting in the physical therapy program, and helping to feed the children.

High school student volunteers might also work with patients who have behavioral problems. In such instances, volunteers may just sit and chat with patients or play cards or listen to records. On occasion, the volunteers may take the patients on a picnic or to a ball game, or arrange some other outside activity. Volunteers in this type of program receive extensive training in how to relate to particular patients and are urged to work with the quiet, withdrawn ones to include them in group activities. Someone on the staff is always available for consultation or assistance, if needed.

As part of the Community Internship Program at the University of Oregon, student volunteers work at the Outdoor School, a summer camp for young people who have attention deficit disorder (ADD), cerebral palsy, autism, or other disorders requiring special needs. Students that volunteer for a special-needs assignment attend a training session that informs and prepares them for what they might face during their experience at Outdoor School. Yet, the experience can be challenging. Chris, a student counselor, explained:

> I was working with Andrew, a kid with Cerebral Palsy who was in a wheelchair. He was a really smart and funny kid. I was challenged the entire week. From the moment I arrived, I realized I was not prepared at all for what I thought I was going to be doing. I had to step back and reevaluate the situation and decide what it was that was going to allow Andrew to have the best time possible during the week. I may have had to do some things that I wasn't totally comfortable with, but by the end of the week, it made it all worth it to see how much fun he had. . . . Saying good-bye to Andrew was

VOLUNTEERS WHO HAVE SPECIAL NEEDS

At the Hebrew Home of Greater Washington in Rockville, Maryland, a group of mentally, physically, and/or emotionally challenged adults and older teenagers—special needs volunteers—work alongside teenage volunteers in a program that has received national recognition. Like many teen volunteers, special-needs volunteers develop useful skills that can lead to paying jobs, according to a report by Hedy Peyser, director of volunteers. The special volunteers "thrive on performing such necessary, day-to-day tasks as folding laundry, packaging slices of bread in the kitchen, and distributing water to residents." For the special volunteers "coming to the Hebrew Home is often part of their daily routine, and since 1976, they have logged more than 100,000 hours of service. These volunteers have found a 'home' at the Hebrew Home, where they have the direction and sense of purpose that are important in life, making them feel useful, accomplished, and necessary—a rewarding program for all concerned."[5]

bittersweet. I was relieved from all my responsibilities, but at the same time, over the week I had been touched so deeply that I know I will never be the same. It brings tears to my eyes just thinking about how amazing the [week] was.[6]

HOSPICE VOLUNTEERS

What is hospice? The term refers to a system of care that aims to keep dying patients in a pain-free, comfortable environment either at home or in a health-care facility, while providing emotional support for the patient and patient's family. The hospice philosophy maintains that dying patients should have the ability to choose the way they would like to spend their remaining days.

Given such a concept, many people ask: are teenagers willing to volunteer for hospice programs? Will teenagers be committed to people who are dying? Will they continue their volunteer work after caring for a patient who dies? The answer to these questions is a resounding YES, provided volunteers have learned to deal with death and bereavement through counselors, social workers, parents, and others who teach coping skills. Proof that teenagers are excellent hospice volunteers has been presented in a number of published articles about Hospice of the Florida Suncoast, where there are more than 200 teenage volunteers who provide "direct hospice patient care in homes, nursing homes, inpatient hospice, and assisted living facilities."[7]

The Florida program began on a small scale in 1994 in a residential facility with 67 beds. Then only 20 teens were recruited, and their training was the same as that for adults, just as it is today. As the program expanded, the hospice staff called on area high schools for volunteers. Staff conduct extensive training sessions for student volunteers and provide support and help in handling grief and bereavement (frequently new emotions for teen volunteers) when patients die. As volunteer Emily Tibbetts wrote:

Before becoming a Hospice Teen Volunteer, I underwent ten weeks of training for two hours each week. During these training sessions, the hospice staff spoke to us about possible encounters we might have with the terminally ill patients. We reviewed the various stages of the dying process as well as the process of grieving that follows. After learning about the potential impact of our volunteer work with these elderly patients, we then made decisions as to whether we would enjoy direct patient contact or would rather do office work, such as filing records or answering the phone. I elected to be a patient care volunteer. . . . Since I have been involved with hospice, I have been given the opportunity to visit three patients in their nursing homes and have been challenged to communicate with patients afflicted with Alzheimer's disease and other dementias. Through volunteering with these elderly patients, I have come to understand the lack of purpose and meaning that mentally confused patients can feel while confined in a nursing home. I have found that I can gain access to the patient's world by attempting to understand his or her mental perspective. In addition to talking with patients about

A PERSONAL GLIMPSE

Teenager Michael Munds of Denver, Colorado, is well known in his city for his longtime fund-raising efforts that benefit a variety of health-care causes. For example, he recently organized a bowlathon for the American Diabetes Association, and in 1996, his bowling fund-raising event raised $37,000 for children who were injured in the 1995 bombing of the Alfred P. Murrah Federal Building in Oklahoma City, Oklahoma. He has also raised money for individual children with serious injuries or disabilities. Munds himself has a disorder known as Treacher Collins syndrome, which causes head and facial deformities. He has had more than a dozen surgeries to correct some of the problems and also must wear prosthetic ears and a hearing aid. But those conditions don't hold him back. In fact, he once told a reporter "I may be at a disadvantage, but I'm not disabled."[8] He thinks that his "disadvantage" may actually help him raise funds for charitable causes because people take note of his unusual appearance.

A MUSICAL GIFT

In Burr Ridge, Illinois, directors of the St. Thomas Hospice Junior Volunteers often tell the story of Patrick, one of their junior volunteers. He was assigned to visit Mariam, a 90-year-old pianist who is blind. Patrick brought along his guitar during visits and accompanied his elderly friend on the piano. Mariam's health improved somewhat and she was discharged from hospice. As a going-away present Patrick bought his friend an electric keyboard so she could play the instrument on the days when she could not get out of bed.[9]

their childhoods, how they have been feeling, and their own families, I attempt to interact with them through activities they seem to enjoy.[10]

Reportedly many of the teens who have participated in Hospice of the Florida Suncoast are far more likely to face death realistically—as a natural part of the life cycle—than do people in the general population who try to avoid discussing or planning for the inevitability of death. As Emily put it: "I have experienced both painful, heart-wrenching moments and joyous celebrations of life. I have come to feel new emotions through entering the lives of several elderly people. Hospice has been important in my life because it has challenged me to serve others, while simultaneously teaching me that 'every day is a gift.'"[11]

Brenda Corace, a former volunteer at Hospice of Florida Suncoast, noted: "Holding the hand of a dying elderly person as he or she peacefully drifts away can change the way someone looks at the world, especially a teenager. I never imagined that, at sixteen, I would share moments like this with terminally ill patients as a hospice volunteer. Little did I know at the time that my experience as a hospice volunteer would teach me so much about life and death, and so strongly influence my perspective on living."[12]

"HAIRY TAILS"

These "hairy tails" are literally just that, but they are also tales of love, and one way to describe a special kind of volunteering. Volunteers donate a part of themselves—their pony tails or braids and other locks of hair to a nonprofit organization known as Locks of Love (LOL), which turns the hair over to a manufacturer who makes custom hair pieces and wigs for young people 18 years of age and younger who have long-term permanent hair loss and cannot afford expensive wigs. LOL determines recipients for hair pieces based on family income.

Only a small portion of recipients are cancer patients whose hair usually grows back after chemotherapy treatments are completed. Most young people suffer hair loss due to alpecia areta, an autoimmune disease. The onset of the disease often occurs in childhood and affects more than 4 million Americans.

LOL accepts hair donations, which must be at least 10 to 12 inches long, cleaned, shaped into pony tails or braids, placed in a plastic bag, and shipped to the organization. "It takes anywhere from 10 to 15 ponytails to make each individual hairpiece," the organization says. Susan Stone, LOL's executive director, notes, "We receive about 2,000 ponytails a week" most of them from young people. "We also have about 500 hair drives or fundraisers organized by teenagers." One drive that Stone recalls was conducted by a student for three consecutive years in her school. The girl "even convinced teachers to cut their hair to encourage the kids to cut their locks," Stone says, adding that she is amazed how young people who struggle for their own identity are "so willing to give up a part of their identity so that another child can reclaim theirs."[13]

Hair donation guidelines are available on LOL's website (http://www.locksoflove.org/).

NOTES

1. Emily Tibbetts, "Learning to Value Every Moment," *Innovations in End-of-Life Care*, 2000, http://www.edc.org/lastacts (August 29, 2003).

2. Anthony Leanna, e-mail to the author, September 1, 2003.

3. Quoted in "Teen Volunteers Learn the Art of Giving," *Healthy Living with Children*, Spring 2002,

http://www.silvercross.org/health_info/newsletters/kids_archive/2002
_spring/art.htm (August 24, 2003).

4. American Red Cross, "Frequently Asked Questions," no date, http://www.redcross.org/sys/search/faqnew.asp (August 24, 2003).

5. Hedy Peyser, "Our Special Volunteers (Not-for-Profit Report)," *Nursing Homes,* March 2003, 37.

6. Chris Basham, "ODS Testimonials," Spring 2001, http://gladstone.uoregon.edu/~cbasham/testimonials.html (August 25, 2003).

7. "Teen Volunteers Help Bridge Generation Gap: 'Patients Just Love Them,'" *Hospice Management Advisor,* December 2002, 139.

8. Quoted in Elizabeth Schwinn, "At 14, High-School Freshman Already Is a Seasoned Fund Raiser," *The Chronicle of Philanthropy,* January 9, 2003, 20.

9. "St. Thomas Hospice Junior Volunteer Program," *Innovations in End-of-Life Care*, July 2000, http://www2.edc.org/lastacts/archives/archivesJuly00/promprac.asp (August 29, 2003).

10. Emily Tibbetts, "Learning to Value Every Moment."

11. Ibid.

12. Brenda Corace, "End-of-Life Care: A Personal Reflection," *Innovations in End-of-Life Care*, 2000, http://www.edc.org/lastacts (August 29, 2003).

13. Susan K. Stone, e-mail to the author, September 2, 2003.

Helping the Homeless, Feeding the Hungry

"Though I live far away from where I volunteered, I realized people everywhere have the same needs I do. . . . I worked with a wonderful group, used my abilities to help others, and learned how people who live in poverty survive."—Canadian teenager April VanAmersfoot, who volunteered in rural Mississippi[1]

Food Banks

Soup Kitchens

Walks for the Hungry

Rescue Missions

Gleaners

Emergency Food Pantries

Homeless Shelters

Perhaps you've seen a few of these terms used in conjunction with volunteer efforts to provide shelter for Americans who have no home and to feed those who are hungry. How can people be homeless and hungry in the richest nation on earth? The question prompts multiple answers, but poverty and lack of affordable housing and jobs that pay an adequate wage are basic reasons some are forced into homelessness and hunger.

⊚⊚⊚⊚⊚⊚⊚⊚⊚⊚⊚⊚⊚⊚⊚⊚⊚⊚⊚⊚⊚⊚⊚⊚

FROM THE BOOKSHELF

Teens with the Courage to Give by Jackie Waldman is part of a Call to Action series and tells the stories of young people who have overcome tragedies and traumas and have made a difference in their communities because of their volunteer efforts. Each chapter is a profile of a young person told in her or his own words, accompanied by a photo and resources for more information.

One of the stories is told by Niesha Sutton, a teenager who eventually became a volunteer for homeless children because she knows what it is like to be homeless herself. Sutton's five brothers and sisters lived with their mom in a rented house in Philadelphia that badly needed repairs but was neglected by the owner. When the roof and ceiling caved in, the family had to get out. But they had no money to rent another place, so they were forced to seek help from the Office of Emergency Shelter Services, which found the family a place to stay in a former nursing home converted to a shelter for the homeless.

Sutton explained how angry, heartbroken, and embarrassed she was living in the shelter. When school friends wanted to visit, Sutton made numerous excuses to prevent classmates from seeing her home. "I would stay after school until 6 p.m. I would sit at the bottom of a hill on the school grounds until every kid was gone. Then I walked home to the shelter. I never let one kid know where I lived," she wrote.[2] Eventually a youth caseworker helped Sutton adjust to the shelter and to become a volunteer helping young children and caring for some of the babies who were there. She found that her volunteer work changed her life, and she vowed to come back after her family moved to their own home. She explained she wanted to help homeless "kids know the most important lesson I have learned. Home isn't really about having a roof over my head. Home is where my heart is—with my family and friends wherever I live."[3]

Other stories focus on youth volunteer efforts ranging from AIDS activists to child amputee programs to youth crime watch.[4]

One way that a university group has helped the homeless is through a container redemption center in New York City. Opened in 1990, the WE CAN center takes in recyclables that poor and homeless people have collected and redeem for funds to support themselves. Containers are sold to a recycler and payments support operation of the center, pay salaries of formerly homeless employees who process the donations, and provide medical and social services to homeless redeemers.

Another effort for the homeless took place in Douglas County, Kansas, during *USA Weekend*'s annual "Make a Difference Day" each October. In 2002, a Youth Volunteer

The WE CAN Center in New York City as it appeared when it opened in 1990. Photo courtesy of the WE CAN Center, New York City.

Council collected winter clothing for social service agencies serving the homeless and other needy people. "It was a lot of work and a lot of fun," said one of the volunteers, Jacqueline Samp, a Lawrence High School sophomore, adding: "We got an amazing amount of donations. Some people went out and bought gloves and brought them to us."[5]

IT'S A FACT

"The number of homeless families with children has increased significantly over the past decade; families with children are among the fastest growing segments of the homeless population," the National Coalition for the Homeless reports. A 2001 survey of 27 American cities found that families comprise 40 percent of the homeless population, and nationally "the numbers are higher." In addition, "research indicates that families, single mothers, and children make up the largest group of people who are homeless in rural areas."[6]

FEEDING PEOPLE

Obesity makes news today, not hunger, and many Americans are unaware or can scarcely believe that hunger exists in the United States. The problem of poverty that often leads to homelessness and hunger seldom captures public attention. In fact, some have called the issue of hungry Americans the nation's "dirty little secret."[7] And there are few advocates for the so-called working poor—those who do not earn enough income to pay for housing, utilities, medical bills, gasoline, car insurance, and other necessities and still have money left to buy food.

However, if you volunteer to work in a food bank, emergency food pantry, soup kitchen, or other program, you will soon become aware of the need to feed people who are forced to skip meals or go without sufficient food for days at a time. In fact, that's how Katelyn in Gibsonia, Pennsylvania, learned about hunger. She went with her mother and their church group to a soup kitchen in Pittsburgh. As she reported in *Teen Ink*

> My mom and I prepared our contribution of food to take to the soup kitchen. The meal was rigatoni with meat sauce, green beans, bread and butter, bananas, cookies and drinks. Arriving with other church members, I could not believe my eyes. There were lines of homeless people waiting for us to bring in the food so they could eat. Each was given a number and when the numbers ran out, the rest were turned away, even if they had had nothing to eat that day. I saw men, women, children,

IT'S A FACT

In the United States, at least 31 million Americans are unsure how or where they will get their next meal. According to a national report on hunger in America, more than a quarter of a million children must line up in a soup kitchen to get food. "The paradox of hunger amidst plenty is a threat to our nation's prosperity and affront to our collective well-being."[8]

"SEWING" GOOD WILL

A teenage volunteer in New York City provides an unusual service for the homeless at a soup kitchen. She's Shifra Mincer, who every Monday night since sixth grade has gone to the soup kitchen at Hebrew Union College, four blocks from her home. At the college, a basement classroom is turned into a dining room each evening. There Mincer, granddaughter of a seamstress, sits just outside the dining room and sews for the diners, repairing pockets on jackets, replacing lost buttons, patching coats, and generally stitching up what needs to be mended. All of her sewing is done by hand. Her efforts have garnered "a lot of friendships," she says.[9]

babies; people of all ages. . . . I hated to see so many people hungry and homeless. I kept looking at the children and wondering where they would be sleeping that night. I felt sorry for the men; they looked so sad and weary. I wondered if they ever saw their families. Some of the men and women commented that they had not eaten in three days. I was shocked.[10]

Another teenager, Jamie Boeri of Devens, Massachusetts, also learned firsthand about hunger in America. Through Youth Against Hunger (YAH!), a community service learning program in Massachusetts, she volunteered her services at a food bank, soup kitchen, food pantry, and homeless shelter.

"Being around people who are knowledgeable about hunger and poverty in our country was immeasurably helpful to me; I learned so much just from listening and watching," Jamie explains on a Youth Against Hunger (YAH!) website. "I felt as though I was really making an impact by volunteering [at the food bank]." Jamie adds: "Hunger is a very hidden issue in our country; it is also looked upon as a shameful thing for someone to be hungry. What many people don't realize is that the people who are affected by hunger look a lot like you and me. Alarmingly, it is a lot easier to become at risk for hunger than many would think."[11]

A PERSONAL GLIMPSE

Abby Weinzer of Phoenix, Arizona, began her volunteer project called Operation Sleep Sac before she entered high school and continued her activities with the operation until she went on to college. The idea for her project was sparked when she was only seven years old and visited a soup kitchen with a volunteer group. "I saw a lot of little children there—three or four years old—hugging themselves to stay warm," she told a staff writer for a weekly newspaper. "They were in really threadbare clothing and I knew that I wanted to help them."[12]

Weinzer's plan was to put together new sleeping bags with stuffed animals and toiletries for homeless children. At first she tried to get donations on her own from sporting goods and department stores, but managers were not receptive and told her she should send a proposal to their main office—where her suggestion might languish for more than a year. Undeterred, she continued with other volunteer work, helping disabled people, which brought her an Outstanding Young Woman Award from the City of Phoenix.

At the award ceremony, Weinzer met city councilman Tom Milton who enthusiastically endorsed her plan and helped to put it into action through a youth services organization. During the first year the project raised more than $10,000, and a camping store sold sleeping bags at cost to Operation Sleep Sac. Weinzer hopes her project will continue for years and meantime she is studying to become a doctor so she can help homeless people with their health-care needs.

Along with Jamie, many other YAH! volunteers collaborate with The Food Bank of Western Massachusetts to serve hungry or undernourished people. One class at Amherst High School, for example, helped out with The Food Bank's Brown Bag Program, which "provides supplementary groceries to senior

Act Now
Organize a group to plant a vegetable garden or fruit trees that will produce food for homeless shelters or soup kitchens.

citizens at 50 sites throughout the region. Students help unload the delivery truck and fill grocery bags the first Friday of each month," according to The Food Bank.[13] In addition Amherst students have held bake sales and other events to raise money for Food Bank programs.

Across the United States, youth volunteers frequently help gather produce for food banks by gleaning—going into fields and orchards to pick various vegetables and fruits that are left after a harvest. Remainders otherwise would be thrown out or plowed into the ground, because it is not profitable to pick them. The produce then goes to food banks or pantries and to other nonprofit organizations that feed the hungry and malnourished.

Collecting canned goods and other nonperishable food items is another way volunteers can get food to those who need it. The collected foods may be distributed to

IT'S A FACT

Some gleaners are guided by the biblical principle "When you reap your harvest in the field, and forget a sheaf in the field you shall not go back to get it; it shall be left for the migrant, the orphan, and the widow, so that the Lord your God may bless you in all your undertakings."[14]

individual families, taken to a homeless shelter, or used to restock shelves at an emergency pantry.

Still other opportunities abound at soup kitchens and other places where meals are served. Volunteer tasks include setting up tables, helping to prepare food, serving at the foodline, cleaning up, and getting ready for the next round of meals.

Be Aware!
If you are assigned to only one job that you dislike at a soup kitchen such as peeling potatoes or washing dishes, you might want to request being given a variety of tasks to perform.

A "HUNGER RESTAURANT"

Numerous international volunteer programs are established to raise funds to fight world hunger and feed people in developing countries who have barely enough food for survival. Frequently these programs inspire individual fund-raising projects such as a "hunger restaurant" set up in a community room of a place of worship, a classroom, or recreation facility. The idea is to arrange the room like a restaurant complete with menus listing meals at various prices, host, waitpeople, and cooks. As "customers" arrive, they are seated, given menus, and their orders are taken. Meanwhile they are shown videos or films of starving people around the world.

Regardless of the food orders, customers are served only a cup of rice and a glass of water and told that millions of people worldwide receive this much or less food per day. After the "dinner" each person is presented with a check for the meal ordered from the menu and invited to pay that amount or a portion of it to alleviate world hunger.

EXPLORE SOME MORE

Many hunger relief organizations maintain websites and a selected few are listed here for further exploration:

Adventist Development and Relief Agency International (www.adra.org)

America's Second Harvest (www.secondharvest.org)

Bread for the World (www.bread.org)

Catholic Relief Services (www.catholicrelief.org)

Church World Service (www.churchworldservice.org)

Freedom from Hunger (www.freefromhunger.org/)

Lutheran World Relief (www.lwr.org/)

MAZON (www.mazon.org)

Presbyterian Hunger Program (www.pcusa.org/pcusa/wmd/hunger/)

Share Our Strength (www.strength.org)

NOTES

1. April VanAmersfoot, "A Life Changing Experience," *Young People's Press*, no date, http://www.pitchin.org/sspeed.htm (September 21, 2003).

2. Niesha Sutton, "Home Is Where the Heart Is," in Jackie Waldman, *Teens with the Courage to Give* (Berkeley, CA: Conari Press, 2000), 32–34.

3. Ibid.

4. Jackie Waldman, *Teens with the Courage to Give.*

5. Quoted in Mike Belt, "Douglas County Teen Volunteers Recognized in National Magazine," *Lawrence Journal-World,* April 27, 2003, http://www.ljworld.com/section/citynews/story/129989 (September 16, 2003).

6. National Coalition for the Homeless, "Who Is Homeless?" Fact Sheet #3, September 2002.

7. Trudy Lieberman, "Hungry in America," *The Nation,* August 18, 2003, http://www.thenation.com/doc.mhtml?i=20030818&s=lieberman (September 1, 2003).

8. America's Second Harvest, "Hunger in America 2001 National Report," October 2001, http://www.hungerinamerica.org/A2H-NatlRpt10-31.pdf (September 1, 2003).

9. Quoted in Marilyn Dickey, "Shy Student Finds Her Niche As Seamstress for the Homeless," *The Chronicle of Philanthropy,* January 9, 2003, 10.

10. Katelyn G., "The Light of Life Soup Kitchen," *Teen Ink,* February 2003, http://www.teenink.com/Past/2003/February/Community/TheLightoLife.html (September 16, 2003).

11. Jamie Boeri, no date, http://www.foodbankwma.org/yah_projects.htm (September 3, 2003).

12. Quoted in Beth Olson, "Young Woman Shows Big Heart," *Jewish News of Greater Phoenix,* June 1, 2001, http://www.jewishaz.com/jewishnews/010601/woman.shtml (August 31, 2003).

13. The Food Bank of Western Massachusetts, "Food Bank Programs: Youth Against Hunger (YAH!), http://www.foodbankwma.org/yah/projects.htm (December 17, 2003).

14. Deuteronomy 24:19.

6

Protecting the Environment and Animals

Volunteers

who are concerned about the state of the earth's ecology and/or the protection of animals are likely to find dozens of choices in places

> "If you believe in something, you have to stand up for it. Don't ever give up the fight against a poorly sited development, pollution, or anything environmentally dangerous. If you do, you are giving up on the world. Even if you don't win, at least you will have tried."—Andrew Holleman, student environmentalist[1]

to serve in their communities. Most cities and towns have recycling efforts; tree planting projects; clean-up and antilitter campaigns; antipollution, conservation, and preservation programs; nature centers; and in some large communities aquariums and zoos that need teen volunteers. In addition, there are regional, national, and worldwide environmental programs seeking help.

So if you are an environmentally conscious person and want to volunteer, where do you begin? One answer might be to check with a local group such as a 4-H club, the Scouts, a city park and recreation department, a garden club, or an affiliate or a chapter of a national environmental organization. Groups may be listed in the phone book or on the Internet.

Each year young people can also get involved for annual Earth Day celebrations, which since 1970 have focused on environmental causes. In addition, National Youth Services Day (NYSD) is an annual event that offers opportunities for volunteering in a range of activities, many of them designed to protect the environment or animal life. For example, 17-year-old Jeremy Drummond of Washington, D.C., began a volunteer group when he was in ninth grade, and for the 2003 NYSD, he and his group cleaned up a local park and planted trees.[2]

In Canada, National VolunTeam Day (NVD) focuses on a common theme each year, often an environmental cause. During 2003 volunteers raised money for a nonprofit organization providing safe drinking water and sanitation services to communities in developing countries. Another project was a fund-raiser for wildlife rehabilitation.

EXPLORE SOME MORE

Some examples of national/international environmental organizations with Internet sites and ideas for local projects include:

- Center for Marine Conservation, which sponsors beach cleanups; Center for Health, Environment and Justice (http://www.chej.org/) which fights toxic pollution;
- Earth Force (http://www.earthforce.org, which sponsors and highlights numerous conservation, preservation and recycling projects that engage students;
- Global ReLeaf, a tree-planting program of American Forests (http://www.americanforests.org/global_releaf/);
- Keep America Beautiful (http://www.kab.org), which conducts antilitter campaigns;
- National Audubon Society, which needs teen volunteers (ninth grade or older) to assist as summer day-camp counselors for young naturalists;
- National Wildlife Federation teen program "Earth Tomorrow" (http://www.nwf.org/kids/kzPage.cfm?siteId=4)

Volunteers often place containers for recyclables in shopping center parking lots such as this one in Ventura, California. Photo by the author.

RECYCLING

Recycling is a popular youth volunteer activity and students frequently start projects or environmental clubs in their schools. You might initiate an activity of your own or team up with an environmental organization, a local government program, a business, senior citizens group, or civic or religious group that has an ongoing effort to "reduce, reuse, recycle"— the well-known recycling slogan.

What can be recycled? Paper, glass, and aluminum cans are the most common items collected and sent to processing centers where they are prepared for reuse in new products. Plastic goods, scrap metals, motor oil, and tires are other types of recyclables.

The most recent efforts to recycle throwaways focus on electronic equipment—computers, monitors, printers, television sets, cell phones, and other items. Teenager Nickole Evans of Tacoma, Washington, for example, is an active member of a computer network in her community that provides expertise in constructing websites. In 2001, Nicole helped the network collect outdated computers and recycle them to low-income families and children with developmental disabilities.

In 2002, teen volunteers in Champagne, Illinois, helped collect computers, monitors, stereos, and gaming systems in a drive sponsored by the cities of Champaign and Urbana, the Champaign-Urbana Public Health Department, and Mack's Twin City Recycling. According to a news report, about 80 percent of the items are salvaged or refurbished. Gold, silver, and palladium from circuit boards are recycled while metal computer cases go to scrap yards.[3]

IT'S A FACT

Electronic waste (e-waste as it's usually called) has become a national problem, because of toxic components in products ranging from computers to microwave ovens. When these items are thrown out they can contaminate landfills with toxins such as lead, silver, cadmium, mercury, selenium, and chromium, which may leak into soil and groundwater. But many states are encouraging efforts to recycle electronic products and attempting to find ways to dispose of e-waste safely.

CONSERVATION AND RESTORATION

What is conservation? In general it means protecting and preserving land (soil), water, forests, and minerals and using these limited and sometimes nonrenewable resources wisely. Conservation also includes wildlife protection and restoration of natural resources.

Tree planting is an important conservation and restoration effort that involves countless volunteers, a large number of whom are students. As you are probably aware, tree planting is the main focus of the National Arbor Day Foundation and its Arbor Day, celebrated in every state each year on a specified date. The foundation also supports yearlong volunteer efforts with programs such as Tree City USA, Trees for America, and Conservation Trees, emphasizing that trees are "vital in conserving soil, energy, water, wildlife, and the atmosphere."[4] Planting trees also helps restore forests and woodlands that have been destroyed or damaged by fire, drought, insects, or diseases.

American Forests and its Global ReLeaf program is another avenue through which volunteers plant trees in towns, cities, and woodlands across the United States. When recent wildfires burned 649,690 acres of forest land in Arizona, the Arizona Futbol Club (AZFC), a nonprofit group that supports the development of young soccer players, along with American Forests launched Wildfire ReLeaf Youth Initiative to help plant trees in Arizona forests. More than 750 soccer players from ages 6 to 19 are participating, with the goal of planting 800,000 trees by the year 2007.

Other types of restoration include national park projects—cleaning up underbrush and trash, repairing benches, building bridges, and restoring walkways. One project took place along the Appalachian Trail in Vermont during the summer of 2003. Six student volunteers from various parts of the United States

TREE PEOPLE

As a teenager, Andy Lipkis became concerned about the loss of trees in the forests around Los Angeles. The trees were dying from smog and other pollutants, and Andy wanted to do something about it. But he was told there was little that could be done. So he mobilized teenagers to plow up an old parking lot and plant grass, then challenged the California Department of Forestry to provide 8,000 seedlings for planting. That was in the 1970s. Since then, plenty has happened. Lipkis, and his wife, Kate, are now the motivating forces behind TreePeople, which has organized volunteer students and adults to plant tens of thousands of trees throughout the Los Angeles area and other parts of southern California.

and two crew leaders from the Student Conservation Association (SCA) built stair steps of granite rock on a low spot on the trail. They used no power tools and pried boulders, some weighing more than half a ton, from the ground with steel bars. Then the rocks were rolled into place, an effort that was more than physical labor; it was also an exercise in building trust and cooperation with strangers. "You have to trust [one another] because if you don't all work together it could be potentially dangerous," volunteer Adam Stepinski, a high school senior from Houston, noted.[5] Conservation volunteers are also involved in numerous community awareness projects to preserve wetlands in danger of being destroyed by pollution or being drained for roadways, housing, shopping centers, or other construction. In addition, volunteer groups help preserve, protect, or restore waterways. A case in point: a group of at least 30

It's a Fact
Each year over 2,000 Student Conservation Association members complete more than 1 million hours of conservation service in the United States.[6]

Members of New York City's volunteer corps who range in age from 16 to 20 take part in a restoration project, clearing an area of underbrush in Morningside Park. Photo courtesy City Volunteer Corps of New York City.

teenagers in the South Bronx area of New York are active in efforts to clean up the Bronx River which runs through their neighborhood. Led by three high school students, Anthony Thomas, Jennifer Reyes, and Divad Durant, the group known as the "River Team," is part of a youth ministry in the local parish. In one project, the activists helped the National Guard pull 44 cars leaking toxic chemicals from the river. The River Team also has pressed the city to allocate $11 million for cleanup of not only the Bronx River but also an adjacent park.[7]

Along with cleanup projects, students from New York to San Francisco, from Minnesota to Florida, monitor rivers, streams, creeks, and estuaries to determine whether they are polluted. Consider Friends of the Rouge River in Rouge, Michigan. Through its school-based program, students learn in the classroom about water quality testing and the watershed in their area. Then they take a field trip to the river to gather chemical and biological data, which may be used to develop river improvement projects. "Some of the biological data is reported to the Department of Environmental Quality. . . . All data received is posted on the Rouge website [www.therouge.org] and shared with participating schools, program sponsors and local communities," according to a report in *River Voices*, a quarterly publication of the River Network, a national non-profit organization committed to solving river problems through grassroots citizen action.[8]

IT'S A FACT

In the United States, "about 70 percent of rivers go untested in a given year even though more than 12,000 student groups monitor waterways," according to the U.S. Environmental Protection Agency. "The involvement of more young people in water protection could make a serious dent in the number of rivers with unknown water quality."[9]

A PERSONAL GLIMPSE

YES! It stands for Youth for Environmental Sanity, an organization founded by Californian Ocean Robbins when he was 16 years old. He says he wants to "awaken the passion and creativity of youth, combine it with the wisdom, experience and insight of elders, and transform the world." Older folks sometimes chide him for his ideology, telling him they once believed they could change the world, too, but then they grew up. Robbins's response: "I'm trying to help us change our definition of growing up, so that it ceases to mean giving up on our ideals, and comes to mean learning how to live our dreams, every day, on the Earth."

Born in 1973, most of Robbins's life has been all about putting his principles into action. According to his biographical sketch on the YES! website (http://www.yesworld.org/):

At ages 14 and 15, Ocean facilitated the environmental portion of two international youth summits in Moscow and another in Washington, D.C. He met with Mrs. Gorbachev [wife of former Soviet President Mikhail Gorbachev] and numerous Ambassadors and U.S. Senators to discuss environmental concerns. His articles began to be published in major national magazines.

At 15, Ocean was co-founder of the Creating Our Future environmental speaking tour, on which he and three other participants spoke in person to more than 30,000 students, presented for 2,000 people at the United Nations, and opened for the Jerry Garcia band in San Francisco.

At 16, Ocean was founder of Youth for Environmental Sanity (YES!), which he has directed for the better part of the years since. YES! has reached more than 620,000 people in more than 1,200 school assembly and conference presentations. YES! has also organized and facilitated 73 week-long summer camps in seven countries, published seven youth action guides, and led 150 day-long youth training workshops. Ocean has spent more than a decade as the primary fundraiser and administrator for this non-profit organization, which now has an annual budget of over $400,000. He has personally facilitated summer camps and workshops in Singapore, Costa Rica, Russia, Finland, Canada, the Netherlands, and across the USA.

Ocean is co-author of *Choices for Our Future: A Generation Rising for Life on Earth* (published by the Book Publishing Company, September, 1994), and speaks widely, spreading a message of hope and inspiration to conferences, companies and organizations.

Robbins currently serves as Co-President of YES! and lives with his wife Michelle and twin sons in the Santa Cruz mountains.[10]

Another example from *River Voices* is a Columbia River project in Oregon called the Salmon Corps. Sponsored by the Inter-Tribal Fish Commission, the mission of the Salmon Corp is

to inspire Native American youth, ages 18–25, in the Pacific Northwest to repair disappearing salmon habitat. Through the incorporation of native languages, tribal environmental knowledge, natural resource management practices, and cutting-edge science and technology into the program, young people are reclaiming connections to their communities, history and rivers. . . . Each year over 100 young adults join the Salmon Corps with a pledge to provide 1,700 hours of service to their environment, their communities and themselves.[11]

CARING FOR ANIMALS OR MARINE LIFE

Among the many ways teenagers can apply their love for animals or marine life is through a volunteer program. Teenager Jessica Quiroz of Oxnard, California, is an example. She says she "loves all animals," and she volunteers at the local Humane League "to try to find homeless dogs a good, loving home." In the future, she would like to become a veterinarian so she can "help all animals. Volunteering is a good experience for me. And I think everyone should volunteer for something. Whether it's helping your neighbor or helping an organization."[12]

Teen volunteers also help out at zoos, usually during the summer. Volunteers may prepare meals for animals and birds, clean windows, conduct tours, raise funds, or assist in corrals where youngsters can pet animals. Volunteer tasks depend on the zoo and its facilities, but, for example, the 70 or more teens who volunteer at the Fort Wayne (Indiana) Children's Zoo for 10 weeks each summer assist zoo keepers or help with education programs. They may work in a replica of an Indonesian rain forest or a section for family farm animals. All the volunteers help out with special events at the zoo.

What other options are available? You can

- Serve at an animal shelter such as those operated by the American Society for the Prevention of Cruelty to Animals, and, if 18 years of age or older, participate in the Foster Care Program to take home orphaned, sick, or injured animals to care for them until they are mature and/or healthy enough to be adopted.
- Help clean up shorelines where plastic objects, fishing lines, medical waste, and other debris endanger marine life and birds.
- Assist staff at an environmental or a nature center, performing jobs that include caring for animals, building bat houses to

protect bats that feed on harmful insects, maintaining bird feeders, cleaning aquariums and display cases for various types of animal life.

◎ Participate in a sea turtle beach patrol or monitoring program along sea coasts, reporting and marking turtle nesting places and other activities to protect these endangered saltwater reptiles.

◎ Create jackets for dogs and cats at animal shelters that say "Please Adopt Me." The animals can wear the jackets for adopt-a-thons.

◎ Promote animal awareness and issues relating to animal protection through school programs.

◎ Collect funds and animal-care supplies for a local animal shelter.

◎ Write letters to members of the U.S. Congress to urge continued support of such federal animal protection laws as the Endangered Species Act, the Migratory Bird Treaty Act, and the Wilderness Act.

EXPLORE SOME MORE

The Humane Society's Humane Teen program website (http://www.humaneteen.org/) provides a place where teenagers post their comments about their volunteer efforts to care for and protect animals. The site also describes numerous student projects in diverse areas of the United States.

Be Aware!
Animal care can sometimes be a "smelly" job and involve such tasks as cleaning up animal waste or maintaining a compost pile to use as fertilizer on zoo grounds or at other facilities.

A volunteer at a nature center may conduct tours and show how living creatures behave, such as this nonpoisonous arachnid—a tarantula spider in a center at Elkhart, Indiana—moving its furry body harmlessly to a youngster's hands. Photo by the author.

Cleaning up toxic medical waste, such as these syringes, is just one part of volunteer efforts to clean up coastal shores in the United States. Photo by the author.

NOTES

1. Quoted in Kathlyn Gay, *Caretakers of the Earth* (Hillside, NJ: Enslow Publishers, 1993), 25.

2. Lynn Minton, "Fresh Voices," *Parade*, March 20, 2003, 10.

3. Erin Podewils, "Drive Recycles Electronic Waste," *Daily Illini Online*, April 22, 2002, http://www.dailyillini.com/apr02/apr22/news/stories/news_story04.shtml (September 7, 2003).

4. The National Arbor Day Foundation, "Conservation Trees," no date, http://www.arborday.org/programs/ConservationTrees.html (September 11, 2003).

5. Quoted in Seth Harkness, "Volunteer Students Moving Boulders to Create Stairs on Appalachian Trail," *The Rutland Herald Online,* July 10, 2003, http://rutlandherald.com/Archive/Articles/Article/68377 (September 5, 2003).

6. Student Conservation Association, http://www.backdoorjobs.com/sca.html.

7. David Whelan, "South Bronx Sophomores Take the Role of Urban Environmentalists," *The Chronicle of Philanthropy,* January 9, 2003, 16.

8. Katherine Luscher, compiler, "Voices from the Field," *River Voices* 12, no. 3 (2002): 15.

9. United States Environmental Protection Agency, "Earth Force Helps Youth Become a Force for Clean Water," *Watershed Events* (Spring 2003): 13.

10. "About Ocean Robbins," reprinted with permission, http://www.yesworld.org/aboutyes/ocean_bio.htm (September 6, 2003).

11. Luscher, "Voices from the Field."

12. Jessica Quiroz, letter to the author, February 8, 2003.

Preserving the Past

While the natural environment takes center stage in many preservation activities, a number of volunteer projects unite nature with history. For example, many

> "Being a Teen Museum Volunteer has helped me decide what to do with my life. I find the museum so fascinating, especially because I get to work with real museum objects or animals every shift."—anonymous volunteer at Turtle Bay Museum in California[1]

American historic sites—landmark buildings and parks—include natural settings that are protected and maintained with the help of teen volunteers. History and nature may be intertwined at history museums or state or local historical societies that need volunteers for landscaping duties and during outdoor festivals celebrating an area's past. And volunteer cemetery restoration projects—cleaning up and preserving burial sites—is not only beneficial for the environment but also beneficial for those who maintain historical and genealogical records.

LANDMARK VOLUNTEERS

The Landmark Volunteer program based in Sheffield, Massachusetts, began in 1990, and offers opportunities for teams of high school students—about a dozen to a team—to spend two weeks working at one of several important historical, cultural, environmental or social service institutions in the United States. Volunteers apply for the limited positions in dozens of locations. If accepted, the teenagers pay their own travel expenses and usually cook their own food for a one-week or two-week session.

The institutions and places where Landmark Volunteers serve are quite diverse. They include

- **Agassiz Village in Poland, Maine, a summer camp for disadvantaged and disabled children;**
- **Colonial Williamsburg in Virginia, one of the most well-known historical restorations of an eighteenth-century village, where volunteers assist with the maintenance and beautification of the grounds and facilities;**
- **International Tennis Hall of Fame in Newport, Rhode Island, where volunteers prepare courts and grounds for summer tournaments;**
- **Shakespeare & Company in Lennox, Massachusetts, where dramatic training and productions take place and volunteers help maintain grounds and build a trail on the property and perhaps usher for some performances.**

According to Landmark's website, the work volunteers do is "primarily manual labor," which may include painting, maintaining buildings and grounds, clearing trails, building fences or whatever tasks are needed to improve a facility.[2] Landmark volunteers, for example, have repainted a full-scale reproduction of the historic Mayflower, restoring its original colors. Called *Mayflower II*, the reproduction was built in England and sailed to the United States in 1957. Anchored at Plymouth Harbor in Massachusetts, the ship is part of the Plymouth Plantation, a replica of a 1627 village that existed seven years after the *Mayflower* first arrived at nearby Plymouth Rock. Volunteers with the painting crew noted that their efforts were appreciated and that "you can really see the effects and importance of our work."[3]

Out west, in a different kind of volunteer experience, Landmark volunteer Loren Wickboldt describes her tasks at the National Elk Refuge in Jackson Hole, Wyoming, on the edge of Yellowstone National Park:

On the first couple of days, we oiled buildings with a brown stain to keep them looking great. After a few days, the group would split in two, one group going to weed. This was not ordinary weeding. We walked four miles one day, through grass up to our necks, carrying pickaxes and looking for one of three thistles in the fields. Working in pairs made the job fun. On many days, we would take turns going to dead fields to move huge sprinkler pipes. The pipes were so big, it usually took three of us to carry them to the semi-truck that was used to move them to a new field. For the entire second week, the group worked on replacing boundary posts. We had to carry all of our equipment up the mountain with us—it was a small mountain—and we would begin our work. After digging four-foot holes with a shovel and a rock bar to break rocks, we would triumphantly place the ten-foot posts in the holes, and then paint them bright orange. . . . Everything we did was hard work, but boy was it fun.[4]

Nadine Kedrus, another Landmark volunteer, worked on the Colorado Trail, noting that her two weeks

were immensely rewarding and memorable. What a group we were! Diverse in interests and backgrounds, our group of 12 teenagers from all over the United States bonded quickly and developed a remarkable esprit de corps.

Hard work was the order of the day—but under the expansive skies and majestic mountains of Colorado—our task was anything but tiresome. How gratifying [it was] to see the results of our labor after only two weeks. Working together under the able guidance of our team leader and Colorado Trail supervisors we cleared and constructed trails, repaired bridges, taking time to relax together—whether cooking our meals, white water rafting or just talking after hours—cemented our camaraderie as well as our bond with the out-of-doors.[5]

Be Aware!
Volunteers are sometimes taken for granted or used unfairly because they often have a hard time refusing to do certain tasks that are someone else's responsibility.

BRINGING THE PAST INTO THE PRESENT

History festivals and special historical events take place in thousands of U.S. communities and probably would not be conducted without the help of teenage volunteers. If history is of interest, you can find opportunities to volunteer at some history museums and historic villages where students are part of living history, playing the roles of early residents and showing visitors how to churn butter, weave, dip candles, whittle wood, make soap, or play a musical instrument. Or volunteers may help maintain buildings, index and catalog for the historical library, tell stories, or guide tours.

History museums frequently need volunteers to greet visitors, take admission fees, answer telephones, help with mass mailings, enter data in a computer, call to confirm group tours, clip newspaper articles about a museum, and answer questions from visitors. In some instances, teen volunteers connected with a historical society may help restore old buildings such as a one-room schoolhouse, a place of worship, or a building designated as a U.S. historical site.

You might also take part in an oral history project for a local, regional, or state historical society, gathering information about the past from people who have lived through specific time periods. Using a tape recorder, you could interview older relatives, elders in private homes or healthcare facilities, senior citizen groups, immigrant organizations, war veterans, people of diverse ethnic groups, and many others. Interviewees may describe their everyday life, families, wartime experiences, work days, travel, or other subjects. Your tape recording may then be shelved in a library or transcribed—put in written or typed format so that a public document can be created. Depositories for oral histories frequently need volunteers to help with typing, transcribing, editing, cataloguing, and indexing interviews for their collections.

Volunteers who "dig" the past can do so literally under the direction of archaeology professionals in a few U.S. sites. An example is the Old Pueblo Archaeology Center in Tucson, Arizona, which has conducted excavations such as those at the

Sabino Canyon Ruin, one of the Tucson area's largest ancient Indian settlement sites, where Hohokam Indians lived from A.D. 1000 to 1300 or later and at the Yuma Wash Hohokam Indian ruin, inhabited from as early as A.D. 750 to as late as 1450. The excavations have revealed underground pithouses, pueblo-like homes, and thousands of prehistoric stone, bone, pottery, and seashell artifacts.

Felina Enriquez and Esther Wilch, recent graduates of University High School in Tucson, conducted an award-winning science fair project in conjunction with Old Pueblo in 2001; they studied corrugated pottery to learn its clay and temper, which is a substance such as sand and crushed rock added to clay to make a pot crack resistant when it is fired. "Studying the clay and temper of pots is one of the most important methods used by archaeologists to determine where pottery was produced, who made it, and what that information implies about the cultural tradition of the pottery makers," according to Alan Dart executive director of Old Pueblo Archaeology Center.[6]

"Old Pueblo allowed us to use their collection of corrugated pottery from the Sabino Canyon Ruins site," Enriquez noted. She and her friend "went through the collection, cleaning and labeling the sherds [pieces of pottery]. We then took the sherds to Desert Archaeology Inc. where we learned how to do temper analysis and ultimately met our project goal which was to identify where the pottery had been made. Old Pueblo was very supportive and because of my experience I decided to declare an anthropology major" at the University of Arizona.[7]

Sara Cermak, a high school community service volunteer at the Yuma Wash site, began her service in 2002 and was somewhat surprised to find that archaeology was not just excavation. Instead she learned that there are many facets to the profession such as detailed laboratory work and record keeping. She liked her experience so much that she volunteered the next year in Old Pueblo's laboratory.[8]

At an archaeological dig in Allendale County, South Carolina, near the Savannah River, 16-year-old Butler Evers was allowed to participate in an excavation. Ordinarily no student under 18 years of age can work on an archaeological site unless accompanied by a parent. So along with his 18-year-old brother, Bennett, and their mother, Beth, both of whom are archaeology buffs, the family worked together to help unearth history. Butler says an archaeology dig is "something I really wanted to do. History is my favorite subject in school."[9]

On the site, Butler dug a narrow channel to divert an expected rainfall away from the archaeological excavation, not a particularly exciting task. However, he experienced the thrill of discovery. While digging, Butler hit a hard object, which archaeologist Al Goodyear, who directs the project, found to be a projectile point used to kill animals. It dated back thousands of years to the Clovis era people, Goodyear concluded.[10]

Be Aware!
A volunteer needs patience and perseverance when taking part in efforts to preserve history, particularly at archaeological sites and in gathering genealogical information.

CEMETERY RESTORATION

Volunteers who want to preserve genealogical records, artifacts, and some of the history of communities frequently go to work to restore old cemeteries, sometimes called "outdoor museums." Markers in a cemetery can reveal a great deal about a family or a community and perhaps even a tragedy, such as

IT'S A FACT

Cemetery preservation websites are a way for volunteers to learn about and protect endangered burial sites. Statewide volunteer organizations have established cemetery restoration projects that include websites encouraging participation. A worldwide site called Saving Graves, which originated in 2000, calls itself "A collaborative effort of cemetery preservation advocates working to increase public awareness and activism in preserving, protecting and restoring endangered and forgotten cemeteries worldwide."

when several children are buried in a single year, possibly dying because of an epidemic. Without preservation efforts, hundreds of cemeteries disappear annually as they are covered over for construction of buildings, parking lots, and highways. In addition when no one is around to supervise old cemeteries, the grounds are often neglected and vandalized. Storms such as tornados and hurricanes may cause severe cemetery damage—toppled trees, broken monuments, and tombstones.

Civic organizations sometimes organize work groups, including teen volunteers, to clean up cemeteries overgrown with weeds, brush, and small trees. One teen group in Bradenton, Florida, the ManaTEEN Club, which has taken on numerous volunteer efforts, began a mapping project in a rundown cemetery. The burial grounds may have been a slave cemetery and is a place where many poverty-stricken people were buried. On the site are crumbling headstones and some markers with no names.

In 2002, club members began mapping out the area to show the location of gravesites they can identify. The map will allow visitors to find burial places of relatives and others. College

EXPLORE SOME MORE

Volunteers working around old graves for extended time periods are sometimes advised to wear protective clothing. Why? Because of possible arsenic poisoning. During the latter half of the 1800s, embalming fluid was primarily arsenic—in high doses. Arsenic does not decompose and could be released into the air.

student Laura Lockwood, who founded the ManaTEEN club in the mid-1990s, said the "Tidy Tombstone Project," as it was called, is "important and fun, but it's also a moving thing to do."[11]

The ManaTEENS drew sections of the cemetery, creating squares for burial sites, filling them in with names when available, then putting the sections together for Manatee County. The project was difficult at times because graves are not in order. But no one was discouraged, and all were confident they'd get the mapping completed. "It's just a matter of getting it accurate," one volunteer declared.[12]

GRAVESTONE RUBBINGS

In some cases preserving history projects may include gravestone rubbings, which can reveal information otherwise not readily available from a weathered or worn tombstone. In fact, for many years, tombstone rubbings have been a way to preserve a grave marker's inscription. However, not all cemeteries allow this practice because of the potential for damage to the stones. But where this activity is possible, the organization Saving Graves advises that rubbings should be made on solid stones *only*—those that are firmly in place without cracks or other surface damage that could destroy a marker when pressure is applied.

To begin a rubbing, the stone should be cleaned with water and a soft brush, never cleaning materials such as detergents or bleach. Never use shaving cream, chalk, flour, or any other abrasive materials on tombstones. Cover the marker with white paper such as newsprint, rice paper from an art store, butcher paper, or pelon from a craft or fabric shop, and secure it firmly with tape. Use rubbing wax, crayons, or charcoal to transfer inscriptions onto the paper or fabric.[13]

NOTES

1. Turtle Bay Museum Teen Volunteers, no date, http://www.turtlebay.org/mtv/index.html (September 17, 2003).

2. Landmark Volunteers, "Basic Information," no date, http://www.landmark.com/basic_info.html (September 12, 2003).

3. Quoted in Jennifer F. Steil, "Volunteers Refresh Mayflower Replica," *The Patriot Ledger,* no date, http://www.volunteers .com/prply.html (September 13, 2003).

4. Loren Wickboldt, "May Landmark Experience," no date, http://www.volunteers.com/meet_volunteer/wickboldt_bio.html (September 12, 2003).

5. Nadine Kedrus, "Landmark Experience: Colorado Trail Foundation," September 2002, http://www.volunteers.com/meet_ volunteer/kedrus_bio.html (September 12, 2003).

6. Alan Dart, "Science Fair Winners Work on Sabino Canyon Ruin Study," *Old Pueblo Archaeology*, Bulletin of Old Pueblo Archaeology Center (June 2002): 5.

7. Falina Enriquez, e-mail to the author, October 6, 2003.

8. "Volunteer Spotlight: Sara Cermak," *Old Pueblo Archaeology*, Bulletin of Old Pueblo Archaeology Center (June 2003): 8.

9. Quoted in Joey Holleman, "Shards of History," *Thestate.com* (South Carolina), May 31, 2003, http://www.thestate.com/mld/thestate/living/5969698.htm (September 13, 2003).

10. Ibid.

11. Quoted in Pat Kelly, "Teens Sift through Time at Cemetery," *Bradenton Herald*, April 28, 2002, http://www.bradenton.com/mld/bradenton/3153290.htm (September 12, 2003).

12. Ibid.

13. Saving Graves, "How to do Gravestone Rubbings," http://www.savinggraves.org/education/print/rubbings.htm (September 13, 2003).

Counseling, Teaching, and Tutoring

"**I** really learned patience trying to get this young boy I was teaching to listen!"

"You learn about yourself, new skills, how others respond to you, what your strengths and weaknesses are."

"I didn't know counseling was going to help me out in school too."

"Most people think honor students do all the tutoring. Not so. Everybody in our club was having some problem in reading or speaking."

"I wish I'd had this kind of attention when I was in the early grades. That's why I'm a tutor."

"It's great to know you've helped some handicapped person learn to swim or do some other activity that you take for granted! I get more out of that kind of teaching than the person who is learning!"

"**Being a student who had once sought help from a peer tutor, I decided that [volunteer tutoring] would be a chance to give something back.**"—teenager Amanda Breuer[1]

These comments represent the views of countless teenagers who volunteer to teach or mentor younger students, young people with physical or mental disabilities, or non-English speakers. In fact, many teenagers begin their volunteer efforts in tutoring programs. Eighteen-year-old Marco Valencia of Oxnard,

Volunteer tutor Marco Valencia of Oxnard, California. Photo by Nissa Beth Gay.

California, is one of them. He says he started as a volunteer tutor during his sophomore year in high school. "At first, I got into volunteering because I wanted to see what tutoring elementary school children was all about, but after awhile I [volunteered] to try and influence someone's life." A member of the school Youth Council Board and co-chair of the School-to-Career Committee, Valencia believes he'll continue volunteering in the future. He can't imagine telling himself "that I had too much volunteer work."[2]

As a tutor or mentor, there are numerous places to serve. Day-care centers or Head Start programs often need volunteer helpers. You might be a storyteller, helping preschool youngsters develop listening skills and imagination. Or you might teach motor skills through games and indoor activities such as doing simple puzzles, and putting together various toys and craft items.

After-school centers need volunteers to provide elementary children with opportunities for constructive play and other activities. In this type of center, teaching goes on in music, dance, woodworking, creative dramatics, sewing, and other craft classes. There may also be home study groups—or a place where volunteers help youngsters with their homework.

Another possibility is a tutoring program for non-English-speaking children. Such a program would offer more than English grammar, reading, or spelling and might include taking students (from youngsters to oldsters) on field trips to increase their awareness of the community outside an ethnic neighborhood. Recreational programs and classes in music, gymnastics, and dance can help a non-English-speaking person gain self-confidence and the ability to socialize with other Americans.

Presenting good safety habits to elementary students is another type of volunteer teaching. Some teen groups, including Scouts, 4-H members, Y-Teens, and high school clubs have created projects that emphasize a particular type of safety each month. In September, for example, volunteers might help elementary students become aware of traffic safety (bicycling and walking). Safety measures for October could emphasize clothing and trick-or-treat precautions on Halloween. In the winter months, storm and fire hazards could be stressed in cold climates, and information provided on how to protect oneself in winter sports. First

A teen volunteer helps a youngster learn about skates and how to use them. Photo courtesy American Red Cross.

aid and fire drills might be the focus in the spring, and summer swim safety could be the pre-vacation spin. Volunteers may use

Teaching a youngster how to fish is just one way a volunteer with organizations like 4-H or Big Brothers and Big Sisters can help out. Photo by the author.

A PERSONAL GLIMPSE

Proyect Amistad, or Project Friendship, is the name of a tutoring and mentoring program that is the brainchild of Los Altos, California, teenager Diana Combs. She initiated her idea as a community service project while a senior at St. Francis High School in 2002. A member of the Spanish Foreign Language Honor Society, Combs wrote the training materials and recruited other Spanish-language students at her school to be volunteers at Castro Elementary School. Working closely with both schools' principals, the volunteers tutored Spanish-speaking second and third graders, helping them to improve their English and reading and math skills.

Combs believes that she and the other volunteers received as many benefits as the children they tutored. "The Castro kids have made an impact on us," she said, adding that they had "built up a great camaraderie." The students, she declared, were "hardworking" and it was "wonderful to see their progress and be a constant in their lives."[3]

films, posters, pamphlets, displays, and other visual aids in their programs and bring resource people—nurses, police, firefighters— into elementary classrooms to speak on various subjects.

Be Aware!
Tutoring and mentoring programs require that volunteers be reliable; those being taught depend on continuity to improve or learn new skills.

Summer camps are still other opportunities for tutoring and mentoring. In Juneau, Alaska, for example, 20 teenage volunteers are counselors at a 4-H camp for youngsters 9 to 12. Campers don't have to be members of 4-H to attend, however, and all the campers have the chance to participate in a variety of activities, such as painting clay pots, making tie-dyed T-shirts, learning archery, making flies from chicken feathers for fishing, and practicing rifle safety and marksmanship. "We keep them busy," teenage counselor C. J. Corso told a reporter. "There's no down time," which is probably an understatement. From dawn to dark, the campers under the leadership of teenage counselors are on the go, whether learning new skills, hiking, performing in a talent show, or playing informal games. One of the adult cooks whose son is a volunteer noted that, "The camp is run for the kids, but I think it's a learning and growing experience for the counselors."[4]

LIBRARY VOLUNTEERS

Learning and growing also occur when teenagers volunteer at libraries. Simone Petche, a Port Charlotte, Florida, library volunteer says she has learned "how to check out books and how to shelve them once they're checked back in." But added to that, she says, is that her volunteer work is helping "me get over some of my shyness."[5]

Teen volunteers frequently help staff prepare and present programs for children. These activities include presenting puppet shows and dramatic plays, face painting at outdoor events, helping children with computers and finding books, and reading to youngsters.

A TURNAROUND

Not every teenage counselor or tutor is highly motivated to teach or mentor. In fact, some teen volunteers are turned off by school and learning, and have been near dropouts or troublemakers most of their school lives. Consider Jim (not his real name). His story is a composite of various individuals who might be called trouble-in-the-making turned tutor-in-the-making. He comes from a neighborhood that social workers call disadvantaged. In most homes, both parents work, if they can find jobs, to keep food on the family table and a roof over their heads.

Jim's parents have had little time or energy for him. There are three other children, two older and one younger. The older sisters are out of school—one quit at 16 to have a baby, the other is a senior but hasn't been able to go to class much because of illness. A younger sister is in junior high, but she is very shy and withdrawn.

Jim has no one in the family with whom he can relate. His father, an alcoholic, spends what leisure time he has at AA meetings, helping himself and others stay sober. Jim's father hasn't had a drink for five years, but Jim can remember countless times when he worried about how they were going to pay the rent and eat with his father losing jobs because of his drinking.

To get attention and have companionship, Jim hangs with a group along a block in the business section where most stores are boarded up. The people still in business there and residents in the apartments in the neighborhood complain about the boys, who yell and tear up and down the streets most of the night. Except for Jim and another teenager in the crowd, all have dropped out of school.

Jim's special contribution to the group is his ability to fix things. He can put together or pull apart bikes (motorized or not), and he can make most mechanical things work. In school, the only class he attends regularly is shop, but that's because he has been involved in a project to show elementary children what certain careers are about. Jim helped build a "teller's window" during a third-grade study of banking. The teacher also introduced the children to building trades through Jim's demonstration.

A high school counselor finally steered Jim into a tutoring program because he thought Jim might work well with Willie (a fictional name), one of the third graders who spent most of his time in the principal's office. When Willie asked about measuring the materials for the teller's window, Jim became interested in the boy and learned Willie needed help with reading and arithmetic. Willie's questions quickly led to a project whereby Jim taught him how to build a doghouse. But Willie did the work, after he read the directions that Jim had carefully written. From this point on, Jim's self-concept began to change as he recognized Willie's pleasure in learning a new skill.

In 2003, teenager Sara Wynhoff in Kailua, Hawaii, created a reading program called Kailua Bookworms in the local library. She considers herself a bookworm and wanted to share her love of reading with children in kindergarten through second grade. "I think this is an important time to show them how books and the library can be fun," Wynhoff said. She convinced eleven other teenagers to help mentor children once a week, either reading to them or helping them to read. The teen volunteers and the young children met for 45 minutes twice a week during the summer. In Wynhoff's view, "a lot of people don't understand that community service is really important and . . . it doesn't take that much time. All these [teen] volunteers are not taking that much time out of their summer, but they're really helping out and making a big difference."[6]

YOUTH COURT

One type of teen volunteering combines some of the elements of both teaching and counseling—and adds a bit more. That's Youth Court, sometimes called teen or peer court. As of mid-2003, there were "more than 890 youth court programs in 46 states and the District of Columbia," according to the National Youth Court Center.[7]

Young people who are Youth Court volunteers serve as the judge, jury, prosecution, defense, bailiff, and jury for juvenile offenders who have committed a misdemeanor or violation. The offenses include, but are not limited to, shoplifting, alcohol and other drug abuses, vandalism and criminal mischief, disorderly conduct, assault, traffic violations, truancy, trespass, and school violations.

If juvenile offenders admit guilt, they may go before a Youth Court as an alternative to the formal juvenile justice system. The purpose of the court is to teach responsibility and hold young people accountable for their actions, thus dramatically reducing repeat offenders. When offenders complete their sentences, they are no longer part of the juvenile justice system. Frequently they become Youth Court volunteers themselves, which helps young people improve their self-esteem and to see themselves as contributors to their community.

Volunteers for Youth Court work under the supervision of legal advisers, law enforcement, social service agencies, schools, or other authorities. They may sentence the offenders to probation, an oral or written apology to their parents or the

Juveniles who have illegally "tagged" (or placed their symbols such as these in southern California) on public and private property may be sentenced by Youth Court to clean up the graffiti. Photo by the author.

victim, counseling sessions on conflict resolution and anger management, and/or community service, such as working in a child care center for disabled children, repairing an elderly person's home, or cleaning graffiti they created.

One teen volunteer who has served on a Youth Court in New York explained how she views her experience:

> I was always the good kid—never tried a cigarette or thought about drugs, and never committed a crime. I always thought that those who did were bad kids whom I would not associate with. Through my involvement with Youth Court I discovered that "bad" kids are a lot like me in many ways—they all think about how they look and what to do on a Friday night, too. The "bad" kids I was so afraid of are really not so bad. They just deal with the pressures of life in different ways.[8]

NOTES

1. Amanda Breuer, "My Volunteer Experience," *Young People's Press*, no date, http://www.pitchin.org/abreuer.htm (September 22, 2003).

2. Marco Valencia, letter to the author, February 10, 2003.

3. Quoted in Amy Goodpaster Strebe, "Project Friendship," *Mountain View Voice,* February 8, 2002, http://www.mv-voice.com/morgue/2002/2002_02_08.mentor.html (September 15, 2003).

4. Quoted in Eric Fry, "Mixing Fun with Challenges,"*JuneauEmpire.com*, July 13, 2003, http://www.juneauempire.com/stories/071303/loc_camp.shtml (September 15, 2003).

5. Quoted in Linda Fudala, "Making a Difference," *Sarasota Herald Tribune*, June 19, 2002, Section B, 4.

6. Quoted in Eloise Aguiar, "Teen Bookworms Share Love of Reading with Kailua Keiki," *The Honolulu Advertiser*, June 20, 2003, http://the.honoluluadvertiser.com/article/2003/Jun/20/ln/ln15a.html (September 15, 2003).

7. American Probation and Parole Association, "National Youth Court Center," no date, http://www.youthcourt.net/national_listing/overview.htm (September 18, 2003).

8. Alyssa S., "Community Service: Youth Court," *Teen Ink,* February 2003, http://www.teenink.com/Past/2003/February/Community/YouthCourt.html (September 15, 2003).

9

Reducing Bigotry, Prejudice, and Racism

One of the most challenging types of volunteer work is helping to reduce the bigotry, prejudice, and racism that exist in daily life. Teen volunteers have been active in

> **"Combating racism is like peeling away the layers of an onion, it can be hard, even difficult, sometimes it can make you cry but if you keep at it long enough you will succeed at breaking it down."— Canadian high school student Terry Bright of Youth Against Racism[1]**

such efforts for years, such as taking on civil rights projects, marching against racist Ku Klux Klan rallies, participating in activities to encourage tolerance and eliminate hatred, joining awareness programs to show the damage that can be done with stereotyping, and putting on events to support gay, lesbian, and transgender people.

Researchers have found that social contact among diverse groups usually helps to reduce prejudice and stereotypes. However, that social contact needs to be a positive experience—without conflict and with the desire to achieve mutual goals. When people from different backgrounds get to know each other as individuals, they may discover they have interests in common and similar hopes and goals for their lives.

Yet getting to know someone who appears different from one's own group is not always a simple matter. In many parts of the nation, people live or work or go to school in a neighborhood where they share similar backgrounds and are of the same racial, ethnic, or socioeconomic group. Or they stick with people of similar backgrounds while they are in school. Teenagers sometimes have to make conscious efforts to be involved in learning and leisure activities that include people from diverse ethnic and racial groups. They may volunteer to be part of a multicultural group advocating unity in their school. Part of that effort could be a "Mix It Up" program sponsored by the Southern Poverty Law Center. The program includes a Mix It Up for Lunch Day and Mix It Up Dialogue Groups. In 2003, a unity group at Chamblee High School in Georgia, for example, promoted a Mix It Up Lunch Day in the cafeteria with flyers and daily commercials via the school's morning news. More than 300 students volunteered to take part. Rather than sitting with friends, students chose places at tables with teenagers they didn't know. "Students chitchatted, joked, and ate lunch with peers that they had never tried to talk to," one of the promoters reported.[2]

On the other hand, Mix It Up Lunch Day has not gone over well in some high schools such as Tahlequah High School in Oklahoma. There only a few students volunteered to change their seating patterns. Why? Some said they could see no reason to sit by teenagers who discriminate against them every day because of their race, religious background, or language difference. Some students thought there were other reasons, such as shyness and fear of someone not like themselves. "People just want to hang out with the people they usually do. It has to do with people's own insecurities."[3]

While a group effort may be difficult to get started, it's even more challenging to go it alone. Suppose, for example, you want to make a difference on your own when you meet a person or several students whose color or religion and social status differ from yours. What if your friends make it clear that they want no part of your newfound acquaintances? Perhaps the group uses negative labels to describe your new friends and insists that "those people" are inferior, not worthy of your time. Your group might even refuse to talk to you if you continue to pursue your new friendships. So you are faced with a choice. Do you give in to the group pressure and exclude a possible new friend from your life? Or do you make your own decision about the people with whom you will associate?

Such questions are even more complex when parents oppose someone not of your own group. Sarah, a teenager in Connecticut, wrote in *Teen Ink* that she invited a new friend home with her to work on a school project and stay for dinner. But Sarah's mother was less than pleased with Carmela, the new friend, telling her daughter that she had a "gut" feeling about Carmela. Why? Because the new friend was black not white. Yet, at dinner Carmela and Sarah's father had a great conversation.

Afterward, when Carmela returned home, Sarah confronted her mother. As Sarah wrote:

I looked at her and said, "I have a lot of respect for you because you are my mother, and most of the time I will listen to you. But you are wrong here, Mom. You have not even given my friend a chance, and you are trying to cut off our friendship because she's African American. Carmela is a good friend, and I'm sorry if you are going to be superficial and only look at what you can see. I am going to be friends with her no matter what you say, because I see more than her skin color."

> **Act Now**
> If you witness a prejudicial or discriminatory act, speak out by saying how you feel about the incident, such as saying you are upset by language or a graphic that insults a group of people.

Sarah noted that she felt "an overwhelming sense of maturity . . . [and] I proved to my mom through my friendship with Carmela that a person's skin does not determine what kind of person [s]he will be. To this day, Carmela and I are close even though she moved back to Alabama. And as far as my mother and me, our relationship is improving every day."[4]

AGENTS OF CHANGE

Beyond their own families or circle of friends, individual teens have volunteered their time and talents to help diminish intolerance and prejudice in their communities, nation, or internationally. One such agent of change is Brian Harris of California, who is featured in *Catch the Spirit: Teenagers Tell How They Made a Difference*. Brian is of mixed-race ancestry, and he and his family have long been active in an interracial group in Southern California. Through this group, he began to speak out about his experiences as a biracial person and was often asked to appear on talk shows and before school and civic groups to share his view about how people of diverse races and cultural groups could get along. He was motivated by his own experience, saying "I know that people of different races and cultures can live together in peace because we do it in my house."[5]

But he wanted to do more than talk about interracial families and being biracial. When he was 12 years old, with the support of his parents, he began a pen-pals club called "Friendship Sees No Color." He noted that "The pen-pal exchange seemed to be the perfect way of opening up lines of

---

SELECTED ANTI-RACISM, ANTI-DISCRIMINATION WEBSITES

American-Arab Anti-Discrimination Committee: www.adc.org

Anti-Defamation League: www.adl.org

Asian-American Legal Defense and Education Fund: www.apa2000.org

Global Kids: www.globalkids.org/index.shtml

National Gay and Lesbian Task Force: www.ngltf.org/main.html

Parents and Friends of Lesbians and Gays: www.pflag.org

The Prejudice Institute: www.prejudiceinstitute.org

Southern Poverty Law Center: www.splcenter.org

Stop the Hate.org: www.stopthehate.org

Tolerance.org: www.tolerance.org

communication. . . . I hoped my project would offer an opportunity for young people, in particular, to make friends with people from different backgrounds." His plan was to have people send him an index card with information about themselves, including their race, plus a stamped self-addressed envelope, and then he would "find someone of one race and someone of a different race, both in the same age range, and put their index cards in each other's envelopes and send them off."[6] To gain publicity for his effort, his family helped him send out press releases and letters to talk shows. Once he appeared on TV, thousands of responses poured in. Throughout his high school years Brian promoted Friendship Sees No Color, and now as a college student he feels that his project has really made a difference in thousands of people's lives.

Another teenager Shawn G. in New York City has also made a difference. He is a Sikh and wears a turban, which has prompted some of his classmates to make fun of him or accuse him of being a suicide bomber. Although it has been difficult for him to speak to others about what it is like to be a Sikh, he writes about it for his school newspaper. "It is strange to see the effect this has on others: their insight changes. My goal right now is to share the beauty of my culture and its people. If, along the way, I can help stop intolerance, so much the better." In addition, Shawn has written "articles for others who feel victimized, to be the voice for students who want to be understood, and help stop intolerance," he wrote. His experiences have taught him that he can be a victim, or he "can be an agent of change. I choose the latter."[7]

Tracy Bray of New York along with two of her friends are teen volunteers determined to make a difference. They founded an Internet group affiliated with Youth Against Racism (YAR), an international organization. The campaign began after Tracy had participated in an online chat and a girl in the chatroom commented about her hatred for blacks. According to Tracy, the girl said she was proud to be a racist, and that prompted other chatroom participants to express their racist views and jokes. To Tracy, the experience was a call to action. As she told a reporter:

"What's our future going to look like? . . . If these kids are already racists, then people are going to be scared to walk out of their doors. . . . The prejudice needs to stop," she said.[8]

Tracy enlisted the help of two Internet friends and using e-mail and phone calls, they began telling others about their antiracism campaign. They also posted signs in their schools to call attention to their message. They meet in a chatroom twice each week. As their website notes:

"We are teenagers out to make a difference. Our voices are going to sing out. . . . Although our title relates specifically towards racism, we are fighting for peace. Freedom from all prejudice. But we cannot do it alone. There is little we can do without the help of adults. We are volunteering. We are not doing this for individual funds or publicity. We are doing this for the good of the human population as a whole."[9]

Another group of student volunteers is also fighting racism, and trying to make a difference in the world. Organized in 2002 at the Foothills Composite High School in Alberta, Canada, the group consists of less than a dozen teenagers, but they have been promoting education about racism as a way to help eliminate it. "Racism is about ignorance, so the more you know, the better we can fight it," according to Lana Selby, one of the two students who started the group.[10] They developed a display that coincided with the International Day for the Elimination of Racial Discrimination. The presentation focused on art, music, and artifacts from countries facing racism issues. For the future, the teenagers plan to hold fund-raisers for Amnesty International.

OTHER GROUP EFFORTS

In some cases, volunteer students are involved with national or state organizations that are dedicated to reducing bigotry, racism, and prejudice. For example, some teenagers take part in leadership conferences and training sessions conducted by the office of a state's attorney general. Not only do teens learn what types of hate crimes are committed in their state, they also participate in interactive exercises that demonstrate how degrading language and slurs can lead to harassment and violence. A Holocaust survivor or bias victim may make a presentation showing how she or he has been affected by prejudice. As part of the conference, students participate in role-playing exercises to learn how to run effective civil rights team meetings.

Teenagers in many schools attend antibias training programs conducted by the Anti-Defamation League (ADL) and its World Of Difference® Institute. Its programs help adults and young people challenge prejudice and discrimination. In fact, a Columbia University study found that volunteer teens who took part in the Institute's Peer Training Programs not only helped others but also experienced great personal development. The study revealed that

- **84 percent of the students reported increased confidence in their ability to prepare and organize a presentation for peers.**
- **86 percent reported greater awareness of their own biases.**
- **86 percent reported a better understanding of the prejudice and discrimination in their schools and communities.**
- **80 percent reported greater skills to confront racial and bias issues in their schools and/or workplace.**
- **75 percent reported that they would now take active steps to confront bias in their schools.**
- **88 percent reported that participation was somewhat or very influential to their involvement in some type of community service in their school or community.[11]**

In 2003, ADL chose more than 100 students to visit the U.S. Holocaust Memorial Museum as part of a youth leadership mission in Washington, D.C. Students of diverse ethnic and religious backgrounds came from such cities as Atlanta, Chicago, Detroit, New Orleans, New York, Phoenix, and St. Louis. During the conference they heard from Holocaust survivors and civil rights workers of the 1960s. For Emily Hom of Tenafly, New Jersey, the speakers were not only inspirational but also helped make the trip a "life-altering experience." Emily said she learned that "we have the power to change things," and that "a little step can make a huge difference." Another

◉◉◉◉◉◉◉◉◉◉◉◉◉◉◉◉◉◉◉◉◉◉◉◉

A PERSONAL GLIMPSE

High school senior Elizabeth Cambers of Mapleton, Kansas, was honored in 2003 for her volunteerism, receiving one of the Prudential Spirit of Community Awards. She had read a story about a little-known Polish woman, Irena Sendler, who rescued 2,500 children from the Jewish ghetto in Warsaw during World War II. Sendler was able to smuggle the children out of the ghetto and found safe hiding places and non-Jewish families to adopt them. She was later captured by the Nazis, imprisoned, and tortured. Both her legs and feet were broken, leaving her unable to walk without crutches.

Elizabeth Cambers was inspired to write a play about Sendler, who escaped the Nazis and is still living in a modest Warsaw apartment. "It is such a story of great courage," Cambers told a reporter. "It occurred to me that our community needed lessons of tolerance, and her story taught great moral lessons."

The title of Cambers' play, *Life in a Jar,* represents the jars in which Sendler placed lists of the true identities of the saved children, burying the jars in her garden. Elizabeth recruited friends to help her perform the drama, which was not only presented at her school but also before religious and civic organizations and educational institutions across the United States. At each performance, Cambers places a representative jar at the door, and audience donations help pay for Sendler's medical care. In addition, according to a Kansas City news report, the script for *Life in a Jar* "has been sent to school districts across the country, and recently Cambers and other volunteers established the Irena Sendler Foundation" dedicated to projects that teach tolerance beyond the boundaries of the classroom.[12]

Tenafly student, Ryan Greene, agreed. "There are small things that make a difference," he told a reporter. "Like stopping someone from using a term inappropriately or incorrectly. Those include racially biased terms, or even the word 'gay'"— such as someone saying "That's so gay."[13]

Along with ADL, a variety of organizations have suggestions for actions teenagers can take to reduce prejudice and discrimination. The Prejudice Institute (PI), for example, begins its advice with "work on yourself first." So does that mean everyone has some kind of prejudicial ideas? Sure. It's common to have stereotypical notions about groups of people—most of us are programmed that way early in life. Yet that doesn't mean someone has to feel guilty about it. Rather, PI suggests looking "for possible prejudices within yourself and for ways you may discriminate without even realizing it."

Then what?

- Be conscious of your discomfort or fear around certain types of people.
- Be aware of tendencies you may have to judge other people because of their appearance, clothing, or speech.
- Take a look at your nonverbal communication with other people. For instance, do you establish friendly eye contact with some people, but tend to avoid looking directly at others?
- Examine whether you equally include people from other groups in your activities such as discussions, group projects, and social events.[14]

NOTES

1. Quoted on Youth Against Racism website, http://www .youthagainstracism.ca/ (December 12, 2003).

2. Chika Oduah, "Come On—Let's Mix It Up!" Tolerance.org, November 19, 2003, http://www.tolerance.org/teens/stories/article .jsp?p=0&ar=75 (December 15, 2003).

3. Quoted in Dana Williams, "Mix It Up at Lunch Hard to Swallow for Some," Tolerance.org,http://www.tolerance.org/teens/ stories/article.jsp?p=0&ar=76 (December 15, 2003).

4. Sarah, "Pride and Prejudice: Prejudiced Eyes," *Teen Ink*, November 2003, http://teenink.com/Past/2003/November/17193 .html (December 8, 2003).

5. Quoted in Kathlyn Gay, *Cultural Diversity: Conflicts and Challenges: The Ultimate Teen Guide* (Lanham, MD: Scarecrow Press, 2003), 100.

6. Quoted in Susan K. Perry, Ph.D., *Catch the Spirit: Teen Volunteers Tell How They Made a Difference* (New York: Franklin Watts/Grolier, 2000), 63.

7. Shawn G., "Pride and Prejudice: Intolerance: 101," *Teen Ink*, September 2003, http://teenink.com/Past/2003/September/16904 .html (December 10, 2003).

8. Samantha Barnaik, "Fighting Racism at a Teen's Level," *Philadelphia Inquirer*, October 9, 2002, http://www.philly.com/ mld/inquirer/news/opinion/local2/4242937.htm?template= contentModules/printstory.jsp (December 12, 2003).

9. Youth Against Racism, http://www.angelfire.com/rebellion/youthagainstracism (December 12, 2003).

10. Quoted in Shawn Britton, "Fighting Racism at High School," *Western Wheel,* Okotoks, Alberta, Canada, March 26, 2003, http://www.westernwheel.com/030326/news-racism.html (December 12, 2003).

11. A World of Difference Institute, "Summary of Selected Findings on Student Involvement," no date, http://www.adl.org/education/edu_awod/awod_findings.asp (December 7, 2003).

12. "Kansas's Top Two Youth Volunteers Selected in National Awards Program," Kansas City *infoZine,* February 4, 2003. See also *Irena Sendler: An Unsung Heroine,* http://www.auschwitz.dk/Sendler.htm (July 30, 2003).

13. Quoted in Joanne Palmer, "'We have the power to change things,'" *Jewish Standard,* November 21, 2003, 7, 41.

14. "What Teenagers Can Do about Prejudice," Action Sheet, The Prejudice Institute, no date, http://www.prejudiceinstitute.org/teenagersFS.html (December 13, 2003).

10

Campaigning, Communicating, and Collecting

Campaigning
and fund-raising
are part of almost
every type
of volunteer
organization or
group mentioned
thus far, and
raising awareness
about a cause is

> "I hope that people will . . . see that THEY can make a difference. All they have to do is try."
> —17-year-old Kim of San Francisco, California[1]

a type of volunteering that involves countless teenagers. A group of teenagers called REBEL (Reaching Everyone by Exposing Lies) in New Jersey, for example, has built a movement to fight against tobacco use, particularly among teenagers, and advocate for anti-tobacco legislation. Sponsored by the New Jersey Department of Health and Senior Services, the group organized in 2000 with a "Kick Ash Bash," designed to develop a youth movement to counter big tobacco companies' influence. More than 350 teenagers, representing 21 counties and ranging in age from 14 to 17, met in McAfee, New Jersey, to launch their campaign. Their message is clear: they will not be manipulated by false tobacco advertising. In their words: "Tobacco companies can splurge big bucks to turn us into their next victims, but we're wise to their lies. We are *Not For Sale*" (REBEL's emphasis).[2]

To spread their message REBEL has held group rallies throughout the state; advocated for smoke-free homes and public places; created anti-smoking commercials for school-based television spots; written and published *REBEL*, a magazine full of facts about the detrimental health effects of smoking plus articles and quotes by teens who are activists in this movement; and developed a website (www.njrebel.com) with lots more information and opportunities for teens to comment. Eighteen-year-old Dee from Eatontown noted:

> I joined REBEL because I wanted to keep people from getting hooked on cigarettes. Some of my friends smoke to "relieve stress." But this is an oxymoron because they may be relieving stress for the moment, but it will give them extreme stress in the future because of the harmful effects of cigarettes on their health.[3]

New Jersey's anti-tobacco volunteer group, REBEL, met at a summit in 2003, and two members presented a "Fight the Good Fight" award to Mike Marts, senior editor of Marvel Comics, for the corporation's tobacco control efforts—its world famous Super Heroes are smoke free. Photo courtesy of REBEL.

REBEL anti-tobacco volunteers in New Jersey gather at a summit in 2003. Photo courtesy of REBEL.

The REBEL campaign has spread across New Jersey, with hundreds of teens signing a declaration, officially showing they are free of tobacco companies' manipulation. In short REBEL volunteers have made a difference in their communities, and according to Dave Bratton, Bergen County Youth Coordinator for REBEL, who works with 15 to 20 high school students, these volunteers have made a positive impact on others, encouraging "teens and pre-teens to live a healthy, tobacco and other drug-free lifestyle." To Bratton this is a remarkable achievement since, as he put it, "High school students are the busiest people on the planet. They have 6 to 7 hours of school a day, homework, after-school sports/activities, perhaps a part-time job, maybe a girlfriend or boyfriend, and their families all pulling their time and focus in [many] directions. The students who give even more from what little time they have are pretty special."[4]

RAISING MONEY

Although volunteers provide much of the free labor and talent to campaign for varied causes, campaigns need money to spread their messages. That often means launching a fund-raiser. Some fund-raisers involve bikeathons, bowlathons, dance marathons, walkathons, skatealongs, road races, telephoning, and mailing out donation forms for dollars. Volunteers might canvas for such organizations as the American Red Cross, American Cancer Society, UNICEF, or United Way, to name a few. Or you could campaign and raise funds for a political group.

Local charitable organizations, religious groups, civic organizations, and school clubs always need help soliciting for donations—whether money, clothing, toys, foodstuffs, furniture, appliances, school supplies, or other items. One type of solicitation began with Aubyn Burnside in North Carolina. In 1995, Burnside (then only 10 years old) came up with an idea to provide suitcases for foster children who frequently have to move from one home to another, carrying their personal things in plastic bags. When Burnside learned about this, she thought "if you're putting your belongings in a black garbage bag, you feel like garbage. I wanted to make them [foster children] feel special by giving them something of their own to keep."[5] So Suitcases for Kids was born. Now this enterprising teenager oversees an organization that has chapters in 50 states and 42 nations and its own website (http://www.suitcasesforkids.org/). On the website you can download a starter kit; find out how to solicit and collect suitcases, backpacks, duffels that donors no longer want and where to take them for distribution—foster care and social service agencies are examples.

Another teenage volunteer, Brittany Ballinger of Portland, Connecticut, conducted a campaign to provide low-income children with school supplies and books for the library in the housing project where the students live. A Prudential Spirit of Community state award winner in 2003, Ballinger had tutored the children, and reported, "I got to know the students and became aware of the lack of resources. I wanted to give them access to resources that would help them in their studies."[6]

EXPLORE SOME MORE

Founding chairman of America's Promise, General Colin Powell, notes that the organization "is about helping kids, but it is also about *young people helping other young people* live full and promising lives." To youth volunteers, he writes: "You are a vital resource in and for your community. I challenge you to realize your potential, take up this cause, and reach out to other young people to make their lives better. Help point them in the right direction. We need your energy, your idealism, and your commitment to help fulfill the promise of America for all of our youngsters."[7] On the website you can read the entire letter and also stories about youth leaders in the organization, whose purpose is to fulfill five promises to every young person: to ensure that each child has the support of caring adults, safe places for non-school activities, a healthy start, marketable skills, and opportunities to serve. Check out America's Promise at www.americaspromise.com.

Campaigning to stop violence is an effort that teen volunteers in diverse communities across the United States have undertaken. Kim in San Francisco, for example, started an organization at her school to raise awareness of violence prevention. Called Step Up Against Violence (SUAV), the organization came about because, as Kim put it, "Every morning when I turn on the TV, listen to the radio or flip though the newspaper, I'm bombarded with news of murders, rapes, homicides, and other tragedies happening in my community, across the nation, and around the world. A lot of it is happening to teenagers and, sadly, a lot of it could be prevented," she says in her message posted on the website SHINE, where teenagers speak out on numerous issues and also can access an Action Guide for volunteer projects.[8]

Stephanie, a young leader with America's Promise, the organization founded by U.S. Secretary of State General Colin Powell, initiated an annual campaign called S.T.E.P., which stands for support, trust, education, and participation.

FROM THE BOOKSHELF

Millennial Manifesto: A Youth Activist Handbook

This book by Scott Beale with Abeer Abdalla is an excellent resource for anyone interested in how the Millennial Generation (those born in 1976 and thereafter) is educating and motivating young people to become activists—in politics and community service. As the authors write in their Introduction: "For far too long, young Americans have been overlooked, undervalued, and misunderstood. An entire generation as been growing up shackled by the stereotypes of generations past and the socially acceptable discrimination against youth. But not anymore. Instead, we are standing up to declare our generational identity, affirm our self-worth, proclaim what issues we care about, and decide in what direction we are taking this country." These words set the stage for chapters that describe the Millennial Revolution, a section on the issues (with a chapter on volunteering), and chapters on youth voting. An appendix includes the Millennial Manifesto, suggestions for youth activism, and advice on how to get involved.

The call for involvement is clearly stated on the back cover of the book: "Our generation has no excuse not to be engaged and work for social change. . . . there are too many pressing issues that demand the creative, capable hands and minds of the Millennial Generation. We must not sit idly by. . . . it is time for us to make ourselves be heard!"

Ten percent of the proceeds from this self-published book go to nonprofit organizations that support youth activism. More information about the guide, endorsements from youth activists and leaders, and ways to use the book for fundraising are available on the website www.millennialpolitics.com founded by the authors.[9]

Each year since 2000 Stephanie has organized a motorcycle ride as a fund-raiser and public relations event called Ride for Shrine. She explains:

> Years ago doctors wondered if I might ever be able to take a step on my own. Without expensive treatments, I faced being crippled because of a genetic birth defect. Without hesitation, the Shriners stepped in to make a difference in my life. For 16 years, Shriners provided me with countless treatments,

surgeries, and ankle and foot braces, all free of cost. Today, I am able to take steps on my own because of the generosity of the Shriners.

Stephanie reports that she plans and organizes the Ride for Shrine, from booking the venue to printing promotional materials to obtaining donations of food, beverages, and raffle prizes from local businesses. Besides the Ride for Shrine, she also goes to schools and clubs to "talk about the Shriners Hospital and living with a disability."[10]

POLITICAL CAMPAIGNING

No politician who wants to be elected to a governmental office—local, state, or national—can campaign without volunteers. In fact, politicians often call volunteers the backbone or the heart and soul of any campaign. Frequently high school and college students get involved, particularly if they are interested in politics, are taking government or

FROM THE BOOKSHELF

Take Action!

Canadians Mark Kielburger, a Harvard graduate and Rhodes Scholar, and his younger brother Craig are co-authors of *Take Action! A Guide to Active Citizenship*, which is a colorfully illustrated how-to book on teen volunteering. The book was inspired by the efforts of young people involved in *Leaders Today*, an organization founded by the Kielburgers and "dedicated to helping young people reach their fullest potential and become socially involved."

Take Action! is full of practical advice for volunteers on how to use the phone; set up a group; conduct a meeting and survey; speak in public; write letters, a petition, and press release; and raise funds. Samples of letters, speeches, and other items are scattered throughout the first chapters. The latter part of the book includes places to get involved and seven profiles of young volunteers who have made a difference.[11]

political science classes or are members of the student government or a political club.

To begin, one of the first organizations to contact is a local political party, which usually has plenty of opportunities to lend a hand. Some possible suggestions:

- Make telephone calls asking voters to support a candidate
- Assist with mailings
- Hold a sign in a public place supporting a candidate
- Put a bumper sticker on your car or in your yard
- Work on a candidate's website
- Help the staff at campaign headquarters
- Conduct research on political issues
- Keep track of opponent's statements and actions
- Take photographs to distribute with news releases
- Work at the polls if a registered voter

REACHING OUT INTERNATIONALLY

Many teenagers begin their campaigning or fund-raising locally, but may soon find that they can reach out on a global scale. Participating in a state or local chapter of Free the Children is one way to campaign and raise funds for an international cause—to free bonded or enslaved child laborers around the world. The organization began when Craig Kielburger of Ontario, Canada, read about the tragic life of Iqbal Masih, who escaped bonded labor in Pakistan.

At the age of 4, Iqbal was turned over to a Pakistani carpet factory to work as an indentured or enslaved servant and supposedly to pay off a $12 debt that his father owed. Like other bonded child laborers in some carpet factories, Iqbal was chained to a loom and forced to work 16 hours a day. He and other children were often starved, beaten, and tortured. After his escape at the age of 10, Iqbal was invited to the United States and spoke to school groups, but when he returned to Pakistan he was murdered for speaking out.

GLOBAL YOUTH SERVICES DAY

A public education campaign, Global Youth Services Day (GYSD) is conducted in conjunction with National Youth Services Day in April each year and is led by Youth Service America (YSA). Steven A. Culbertson, president of YSA says "Countries around the world are beginning to recognize children and teenagers as assets, tapping into their amazing energy, commitment, and idealism to solve problems. Despite escalating violence around the world, young volunteers from different geographic, socioeconomic, ethnic, and religious backgrounds are organizing service projects, public awareness campaigns and forums that tackle some of society's most intractable problems while promoting dialogue and tolerance."[12]

Since the first GYSD in 2000, international organizations such as the Habitat for Humanity International, Peace Corps, United Nations, and YMCA International have joined YSA to expand the GYSD program. "Youth play a special role in fostering the spirit of hope necessary to make the world a better place," according to Timothy E. Wirth, president of United Nations Foundation and Better World Fund. "Global Youth Service Day is a remarkable initiative because it channels the passion and dedication of youth in addressing the world's challenges, not only for one day, but for a lifetime."[13]

A 1995 news story of Iqbal's death prompted Kielburger, then only 12 years old, to begin his crusade Kids Can, now called Free the Children. Since then, he has spoken to countless local, national, and international groups. As a result, hundreds of thousands of young people in the United States and dozens of other nations have taken part in fund-raising activities for Free the Children. The funds pay for school construction, school kits, medical supplies, and water projects in developing countries. The rapid growth and dramatic achievements of Free the Children are described in Kielburger's book by the same title (published by HarperCollins) and the organization's website (http://www.freethechildren.org/main/whatisftc 1b.htm).

Another way to become internationally involved is through People to People International (PTPI), with headquarters in Kansas City, Missouri. In 2003, PTPI initiated a peace camp, which is designed to be an annual event for youth delegates between the ages of 14 and 18.

The first camp was held in Egypt, and brought together young people of diverse nationalities and religions from various regions of the world, including 25 delegates from the United States. Teenagers were able to freely express their views and at the same time learn valuable communication skills as well as develop empathy and understanding for one another. They also took part in workshops and activities to find realistic ways to understand today's global problems and take constructive ideas back to their own countries to share with others.[14]

Another international opportunity could be with Global Volunteers, a nonprofit organization based in St. Paul, Minnesota. Founded in 1984, Global Volunteers (GV) sponsors short-term work projects in about 19 countries. Indigenous host groups request help, and GV sends teams to a country to construct community buildings, work at health-care clinics, dig wells, erect street signs, install playground equipment, work in nature reserves, plant crops, and teach conversational English to students of all ages.

Volunteers may be high school or college students, but minors must be accompanied by their parents or guardians, and families are encouraged to participate. Not only do volunteers provide their services but they also pay their own transportation to the project site. In addition, they pay a fee, which can range from several hundred dollars to several thousand dollars, to support the local development program and cover the costs of food, lodging, project materials, ground transportation, and the services of a team leader.

NOTES

1. Kim, "Step Up Against Violence," *SHINE,* no date, http://www.shine.com/action_takeastand.cfm?content_id=school_violence (October 3, 2003).

2. Amanda Feldman and Stephanie Marguglio, "They May Try to Define Us . . . but We Are Not for Sale," *REBEL: An Advocacy Magazine Written by TEENS for Teens* 2.

3. REBEL, "The Low Down—Real Stories—Dee, 18, Eatontown, NJ," http://www.njrebel.com/low_down/real_stories_dee.asp (December 15, 2003).

4. David Bratton, e-mail correspondence with the author, December 26, 2003.

5. Quoted in Domenica Marchetti, "Charity's Youth Movement," *The Chronicle of Philanthropy,* January 9, 2003, 7.

6. Quoted in Prudential Financial, "State Honorees," 2003, http://www.prudential.com/productsAndServices/0,1474,intPageID%253D1631%2526blnPrinterFriendly%253D0,00.html (September 18, 2003).

7. General Colin L. Powell, "General Powell's Message to Youth," no date, http://www.americaspromise.com/about/message_youth.cfm (September 19, 2003).

8. Kim, "Step Up Against Violence," SHINE, no date, http://www .shine.com/action_takeastand.cfm?content_id=school_violence. See also SHINE's Action Guide, http://www.shine365.com/action_guide .cfm (October 3, 2003).

9. Scott Beale with Abeer B. Abdalla, *Millennial Manifesto: A Youth Activist Handbook by, for, and about the Millennial Generation* (Scott Beale, 112 Ben Lane, Newark, DE 19711, 2003).

10. Stephanie, America's Promise, "Meet a Leader," no date, http:// www.americaspromise.com/youth/inspired/stephanie.cfm (December 17, 2003).

11. Marc Kielburger and Craig Kielburger, *Take Action! A Guide to Active Citizenship* (Hoboken, NJ: John Wiley & Sons, 2002).

12. "In a World at War, Millions of Young People Come Out to Volunteer for Peace," press release, April 8, 2003.

13. Timothy E. Wirth, "Quotes," Global Youth Services Day 2003, http://www.gysd.net/home/index.html?width=800 (September 20, 2003).

14. People to People International, "PTPI Initiates Youth Peace Camp," press release, May 1, 2003.

11

Getting Started, Reaping Rewards

If the stories you've read about youth volunteers have inspired you to become involved in some type of service and you have never been a volunteer, where do you

> Volunteering "makes you realize life just ain't about smoking weed and sitting around. There are other things to do, and you can make money legally."—17-year-old volunteer at a Sears Youth Center, a rehabilitation facility for youthful offenders in Missouri. Another Center volunteer adds: Volunteering "gives us a chance to gain the respect of the community. And it's fun."[1]

begin? It's a logical question with as many different answers as there are people who decide to volunteer. Perhaps one of the first steps is to determine what motivates you. Do you want to meet new people? Make a difference in your own community? Learn new skills? Gain experience for a college application or a job? Go on an adventure? Build your self-esteem?

Questions should also focus on your personal interests. Would you like to volunteer with a local group that provides services for seniors? Do you want to help the ill, abused, disabled, homeless, or hungry? Do you want to protect animals? Are you an environmentalist? Do you have a talent for teaching, coaching, or mentoring? Are you artistic and able to design posters, brochures, or other graphics for fund-raising campaigns? Do you have computer skills to help set up or maintain websites for volunteer groups?

Other factors to consider are whether you want to work one-on-one with individuals or with a group; whether you like to be out in the public or work behind the scenes; whether you want to make a long-term or short-term commitment. Another factor could be transportation—your ability to get to the place where you plan to volunteer.

WHAT NEXT?

Once you've decided what type of volunteer work you'd like to do, the next step would be to check out the prospects available. Perhaps a service-learning course already offers places to serve. Teachers and counselors and student coordinators may have a directory of opportunities, or these may be posted on a community service bulletin board.

You can also check out a few organizations that meet your interests and ask them about their mission and how they serve. In short, interview the organization so you can find out whether it's where you want to volunteer.

Be Aware!
You don't have to volunteer for the first organization you interview; if you don't find it appealing, try another.

Another option is the website VolunteerMatch (www .volunteermatch.org), which claims to be "the web's largest data base of volunteer opportunities." Once you've accessed the site, you can enter your zip code and then click on the "search" button. A list of opportunities in your area will appear—those with a "T" symbol indicate teenagers can apply. After selecting a place of interest—perhaps Big Brothers and Big Sisters—you can then click on that link and learn what the volunteer hours are and the address. If the opportunity appeals, the next step is to click on the box titled "I Like This Opportunity" and fill out the form

---

IT'S A FACT

One study of volunteers found that 60 percent of teenagers get involved in service activities through their places of worship, while 28 percent go through their school programs. Other teen connections occur through service clubs or volunteer organizations.[2]

---

that appears. The e-mail form goes to the organization seeking volunteers, and the organization in turn contacts you about their program. VolunteerMatch also has links to local affiliates of national organizations, nonprofit partners, and Volunteer FAQs.

ON YOUR OWN

Perhaps you see a need in your community that no one else has recognized, and you've thought of a project that you'd like to initiate on your own. If you are the type that takes the lead, you could begin canvassing your friends, neighbors, and others to bring them together for an action project. Find out what their interests and talents are and how they would fit into plans for serving your community. Get the support of a few people who can advise, act as consultants, and open doors to resources and organizations that might help.

FROM THE BOOKSHELF

The Complete Idiot's Guide to Volunteering for Teens

Of course, the author of this guide, Preston Gralla, does not assume anyone who reads the book is an "idiot." This is one of many books in the "Complete Idiot Guide" series, and it provides numerous volunteering how-tos, from preparing for volunteer experiences to finding opportunities.[3]

Be Aware!
Going it alone can be a discouraging process at times because people you contact to help are not as interested or as passionate about a cause as you are. Still a positive attitude and persistence usually pay off, helping you get a project started and running.

Once your group is formed, you'll need to clearly define your purpose for getting together and then determine what type of project will fulfill that purpose. Suppose, for example, you are concerned about an alarming number of child drownings in a river that runs through your town. Your group's purpose would be to prevent such tragic accidents. Maybe your project would be an educational program in elementary schools to warn youngsters of dangerous waterways and teach them how to save themselves in deep water. A popular project is a campaign to raise awareness of alcohol and other drug abuse or health issues that affect teens especially. Hundreds of other ideas can be found on Internet websites of the organizations listed in the appendix and in the publications described in this book.

Finally, as Craig Kielburger writes in his book about volunteering, "Every one of us is born with special gifts or talents. And as young people, it is both our right and our responsibility to use these talents to help find solutions to problems affecting our world. . . . All we have to do is believe that we can make a difference, and we will."[4]

NOTES

1. Quoted in Lindsay Cummings, "Sears Youth Volunteerism Is Recognized," *Daily American Republic*, September 8, 2003, http://www.darnews.com/articles/2003/09/08/news/news17.txt (September 29, 2003).

2. Peggy Patten, "Volunteerism and Youth: What Do We Know?" *Parent News Online*, January-February 2000, http://npin .org/pnews/2000/pnew100/spot100.html (September 25, 2003).

3. Preston Gralla, *The Complete Idiot's Guide to Volunteering for Teens* (Indianapolis, IN: Alpha Books/Pearson Education, 2001).

4. Mark Kielburger and Craig Kielburger, *Take Action! A Guide to Active Citizenship* (Hoboken, NJ: John Wiley & Sons, 2002), vi.

5. David Bratton, e-mail to the author, December 26, 2003.

YOU CAN QUOTE THEM

"[Teenagers] who volunteer their time, who at a young age care so much about helping others, are anything but standard. They are exceptional and extraordinary. They live the concept [of altruism] . . . at that time of their life, when popularity is paramount and life is all about 'me,' to see beyond themselves and to dedicate themselves to a greater good that even some adults can't see or willfully ignore, well that's amazing."—David Bratton, Bergen County Youth Coordinator for REBEL, the New Jersey (statewide) teen anti-smoking group[5]

"Teens who volunteer increase their knowledge of the world and the problems that face it. Volunteering affords teens both an opportunity to shape their communities and to receive lifelong personal benefits. Furthermore, formal and informal volunteer experiences during teen years increase the possibility of continued volunteering in adulthood. Teen volunteering provides positive experiences for youth, benefits society, and establishes a foundation for lifelong civic duty."—Matthew Hamilton and Afshan Hussain, eds., *America's Teenage Volunteer*[6]

"Like those who came before them, America's young people have time and talents that they can share with those in need. In the process of serving others, they will be helping communities, developing their personal characters, and learning about our civic traditions and institutions."—President George W. Bush[7]

"Youth volunteers . . . are doing more for their communities than ever before. Their acts of commitment and devotion are truly remarkable and should be valued by all."—Dina Formentini, Pinellas County Extension[8]

"Today's youth recognize the benefits of volunteering for their communities as well as themselves, and we can help plant the seeds of lifelong community service by introducing them to volunteer opportunities when they are young."—Steven A. Culbertson, president and CEO Youth Service America[9]

"Young adults are enthusiastic about an expanded AmeriCorps type program—where every young person would be offered a chance to do a full year of community service to earn money for tuition."—CIRCLE[10]

"[V]olunteerism no longer merely means, 'giving back to the community'—it has increasingly become a form with which to change and shape society in positive ways. Service, whether in the context of the military, the community, or the school, has political implications as one of the most important issues of our generation."—Scott Beale, co-founder Millennial Politics[11]

6. Matthew Hamilton and Afshan Hussain, eds., *America's Teenage Volunteer*, booklet (Washington, DC: Independent Sector, no date), no page number.

7. George W. Bush in an introductory letter for *Students in Service to America: A Guidebook for Engaging America's Students in a Lifelong Habit of Service*, April 24, 2002, 1.

8. Dina Formentini, "Timely Topics," Pinellas County Extension, August 2, 2002, http://coop.co.pinellas.fl.us/TimeTweb/2002/august02/augyouthmapping.htm (October 5, 2003).

9. Steven A. Culbertson, January 30, 2003, http://www .kohlscorporation.com/2003PressReleases/News0130Release.htm (October 5, 2003).

10. CIRCLE, "Volunteering/Community Service," no date, http://www.civicyouth.org/quick/volunteer.htm (October 5, 2003).

11. Scott Beale with Abeer B. Abdalla, founders of Millennial Politics, in *Millennial Manifesto: A Youth Activist Handbook by, for, and about the Millennial Generation* (Scott Beale, 112 Ben Lane, Newark, DE 19711, 2003), 41–42.

Selected Resource Organizations

American Red Cross
Program and Services Department Youth Associate
431 18th Street NW
Washington, DC 20006
www.redcross.org/services/youth/0,1082,0_326_,00.html
The American Red Cross provides young people with
meaningful opportunities for education, training, and
volunteer/community service. Forty percent of all Red Cross
volunteers are young people up to age 24.

America's Promise
909 N. Washington Street, Suite 400
Alexandria, VA 22314
www.americaspromise.org
America's Promise/Alliance for Youth says it mobilizes "people
from every sector of American life to build the character and
competence of our nation's youth by fulfilling Five Promises:
ongoing relationships with caring adults, safe places with
structured activities, a healthy start, marketable skills, and
opportunities to give back."

AmeriCorps
Corporation for National and Community Service
1201 New York Avenue NW
Washington, DC 20525
www.americorps.org
A program of the Corporation for National and Community
Service, AmeriCorps is a network of national service programs
that engages people 17 and older in service to their community.
For a term of service with AmeriCorps, members can earn an
education award up to $4,725 that can be used for student loan
repayment and school tuition.

Boy Scouts of America
1325 West Walnut Hill Lane
Irving, TX 75015-2079
www.scouting.org
Boy Scouts of America is an educational program for boys and
young adults helping to build character and receive training in
the responsibilities of participating citizenship.

Boys and Girls Clubs of America
1230 West Peachtree Street NW
Atlanta, GA 30309-3447
www.bgca.org
Teenagers can take part in club programs and services that
"promote and enhance the development of boys and girls by
instilling a sense of competence, usefulness, belonging and
influence."

Campus Outreach Opportunity League (COOL)
1531 P Street NW, Suite LL
Washington, DC 20005
www.cool2serve.org
COOL states that its mission is "to educate, connect and
mobilize college students and their campuses to strengthen
communities through service and action."

Center for Information and Research (CIRCLE)
www.civicyouth.org/quick/volunteer.htm
The website for CIRCLE provides access to statistics about youth volunteering and describes the research that it conducts and funds and the projects it supports to increase the engagement of young people between the ages of 15 and 25 in politics and civic life.

City Year
285 Columbus Avenue
Boston, MA 02116
www.city-year.org
The City Year motto is "Young Enough to Want to Change the World, Old Enough to Do It." This diverse group of young people (17 to 24 years old) unites for a year of full-time, rigorous community service, leadership development, and civic engagement.

Congressional Award Foundation
P.O. Box 77440
Washington, DC 20013
www.congressionalaward.org
The U.S. Congress established this award program for young people, 14 to 23 years old, who set goals to earn medals in four program areas: volunteer public service, personal development, physical fitness, and expedition/exploration.

Do Something
423 West 55th Street, 8th Floor
New York, NY 10019
www.dosomething.org
Helps teens get involved in service in their communities and posts essays, poetry, and artwork by youth.

Earth Force
1908 Mt. Vernon Avenue, Second Floor
Alexandria, VA 22301
www.earthforce.org
This organization helps young people discover and implement lasting solutions to environmental issues in their community.

EXCEL Clubs
National Exchange Club
3050 Central Avenue
Toledo, OH 43606-1700
www.nationalexchangeclub.com/ProgramsService/excel_clubs.
htm
Chartered under the National Exchange Club, EXCEL Clubs
are "groups of high school students dedicated to improving
their schools, communities and country through volunteerism."

Girl Scouts of the U.S.A.
420 Fifth Avenue
New York, NY 10018-2702
www.girlscouts.org
Through five age levels of programs, including Senior Girl
Scouts aged 14 to 17, girls learn leadership and decision-
making skills and ways to serve their communities.

Habitat for Humanity International
121 Habitat Street
Americus, GA 31709
www.Habitat.org
This nonprofit, ecumenical Christian housing ministry "seeks
to eliminate poverty housing and homelessness from the world,
and to make decent shelter a matter of conscience and action."

Hugh O'Brian Youth Leadership (HOBY)
10880 Wilshire Boulevard, Suite 410
Los Angeles, CA 90024
www.hoby.org
HOBY says its "mission is to seek out, recognize and develop
leadership potential commencing with high school
sophomores." Young people meet with recognized civic leaders
and attend seminars at the community, state, and international
levels. "Participants are expected to provide at least one
hundred hours of service."

Internet Nonprofit Center
The Evergreen State Society
P.O. Box 20682
Seattle, WA 98102-0682
www.nonprofits.org
This online center provides information and advice about
nonprofit organizations and volunteering.

Key Club International
3636 Woodview Trace
Indianapolis, IN 46268
www.keyclub.org/keyclub
"Key Club is the oldest and largest service program for high
school students," and its success is attributed to the fact that it
is a student-led organization that teaches leadership through
serving others.

Kids for a Clean Environment (F.A.C.E.)
P.O. Box 158254
Nashville, TN 37215
www.kidsface.org
This organization provides information on environmental
issues to young people and encourages youth to be involved
with action programs that benefit the environment.

National 4-H
Families, 4-H & Nutrition
CSREES/USDA
1400 Independence Avenue SW
Washington, DC 20250-2225
www.4-H.org
4-H clubs are part of the youth education branch of the
Cooperative Extension Service, U.S. Department of Agriculture.
A County Extension office provides access to both youth and
adult programs.

National Youth Leadership Council
1667 Snelling Avenue N
St. Paul, MN 55108
www.nylc.org/index.cfm
The National Youth Leadership Council is a clearinghouse for information about service-learning.

Network for Good
www.networkforgood.org/volunteer/index.html
This nonprofit organization makes use of the Internet to encourage people to volunteer, raise funds, and speak out about issues that concern them. There is access to an online community of young people called YouthNOISE. Youth worldwide work together "to make NOISE about things they don't like, take ACTION on issues that matter to them and make a DIFFERENCE in the lives of young people everywhere."

Pitch In
Young People's Press
110 Eglinton Avenue W, Suite 200
Toronto, ON M4R 1A3
www.pitchin.org/intro.htm
An e-zine originating in Canada that focuses on experiences of teen volunteers described in their own words.

Points of Light Foundation
1400 I Street NW, Suite 800
Washington, DC 20005
www.pointsoflight.org
The Points of Light Foundation & Volunteer Center National Network is an organization that mobilizes volunteers—young and old and all walks of life—to help solve serious social problems through a variety of programs and services.

The Prejudice Institute
2743 Maryland Avenue
Baltimore, MD 21218
http://www.prejudiceinstitute.org
The Prejudice Institute is a nonprofit, nonpartisan organization
devoted to policy research and education on all dimensions of
prejudice, discrimination, and ethnoviolence.

Prudential Spirit of Community Initiative
The Prudential Insurance Company of America
751 Broad Street
Newark, NJ 07102-3777
www.prudential.com/community
Sponsored by Prudential Financial Services, the Prudential
Spirit of Community Initiative recognizes students at the local,
state, and national levels for their commendable community
service that they have initiated.

Save the Children
54 Wilton Road
Westport, CT 06880
www.savethechildren.org
A member of the International organization, Save the Children
encourages volunteers to raise funds for children in crisis
worldwide.

Students Against Destructive Decisions (SADD)
SADD National
Box 800
Marlborough, MA 01752
www.saddonline.com
This youth organization uses peer influence to spread the
message of positive decision making and promotes a "no-use"
policy regarding underage drinking, impaired driving, drug use,
violence, and suicide.

Teens, Crime, and the Community
c/o Street Law, Inc.
1600 K Street NW, Suite 602
Washington, DC 20006
www.nationaltcc.org
This national program helps teens get involved in crime prevention, and a special teens page tells how to start a youth safety corps club, includes stories about what youth are doing to stop crime in their communities, and describes various action projects.

Voices of Youth
www.unicef.org/voy
This is a website that encourages youth discussions of important world issues and suggests ideas on how this world can become a place where children can live in peace, have decent and healthy places to live, get an education, and be protected from violence and exploitation.

VolunteerMatch
www.volunteermatch.org
This nonprofit, online service helps people quickly find local volunteer opportunities matching their individual interests and schedules.

Volunteers of America, Inc.
110 S. Union Street
Alexandria, VA 22314
www.voa.org
This organization declares that it is a "national, nonprofit, spiritually based organization providing local human service programs and opportunities for individual and community involvement."

YMCA of the USA
101 North Wacker Drive
Chicago, IL 60606
www.ymca.net
YMCA "Leaders Clubs involve teens in community service projects. In Youth and Government, hands-on activities teach them about state government."

Youth Activism Project (formerly Activism 2000 Project)
P.O. Box E
Kensington, MD 20895
www.youthactivism.com/
A private nonpartisan organization to encourage young people to speak up and pursue lasting solutions to problems they care deeply about.

Youth as Resources
Center for Youth as Resources
1700 K Street NW, Suite 801
Washington, DC 20006
www.yar.org
Provides small grants to young people who want to design and carry out service projects.

Youth Crime Watch of America
9300 S. Dadeland Boulevard, Suite 100
Miami, FL 33156
www.ycwa.org
This youth-led organization and movement is an effort to create a crime-, drug-, and violence-free environment in schools and neighborhoods.

Youthlink
www.youthlink.org
This former site for the Global Youth Action Network is now the site for Youth in Action, which is "dedicated to creating support and recognition for the voices, ideas and positive contributions of young people. Its programs are focused on improving citizenship, civic engagement and communities through youth leadership and positive action." A "Youth Action Guide" can be downloaded from this site.

Youth Service America
1101 15th Street NW, Suite 200
Washington, DC 20005
www.ysa.org
This organization's motto is "Making Service and Service-Learning the Common Expectation and Common Experience of All Young People in America." It is a resource center in partnership with "thousands of organizations committed to increasing the quantity and quality of opportunities for young Americans . . . to serve locally, nationally, or globally."

Youth Venture National Office
1700 N. Moore Street, Suite 2000
Arlington, VA 22209
www.youthventure.org
Young people are in charge of this organization, which "empowers [them] to create and launch their own enterprises, and through these enterprises, to take greater responsibility for their lives and communities."

Youth Volunteer Corps of America
4600 W. 51st Street, Suite 300
Overland Park, KS 66205
www.yvca.org
Through this organization, young people can find ways to help others and how to participate in service projects.

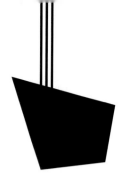

Index

Index

About the Author

Kathlyn Gay is the author of more than one hundred books that focus on social and environmental issues, culture, history, communication, and sports for a variety of audiences. Some of her books have been written in collaboration with family members. A full-time freelance author, Kathlyn has also published hundreds of magazine features and stories, plays, and promotional materials, and she has written and contributed to encyclopedias, teachers' manuals, and textbooks. She and her husband, Arthur, are Florida residents.